B+T
6.95
30Jan'80

WHAT CAN GOD DO?

What Can God Do?

FREDERICK SONTAG

NASHVILLE   ABINGDON

What Can God Do?

Library of Congress Cataloging in Publication Data

Sontag, Frederick.
  What can God do?
  1. God—Attributes. I. Title.
BL205.S67   231'.4   79-4352

ISBN 0-687-44600-7

MANUFACTURED BY THE PARTHENON PRESS AT
NASHVILLE, TENNESSEE, UNITED STATES OF AMERICA

For
ACF and VRF
and their family

Happy are those who love you,
happy those who rejoice over
your peace.

Tobit 13:14
(The Jerusalem Bible)

CONTENTS

WHAT CAN GOD DO?

PREFACE

We finally come to know ourselves, and others, when we learn what we can and cannot do. There is no reason why our way of knowing God should be any different. If anyone denies God's existence, he or she is actually denying that we have any knowledge of what God can and cannot do. By the same reasoning, to learn about God is to discover both his powers and his limitations. **We begin to form our picture of how God can be present and absent to us when we realize what he can and what he cannot do.** It does not matter whether these limitations are inherent in his nature or freely self-imposed.

Of course, to come to know God is a more difficult task than to understand either yourself or another person. At least, we human beings can see each other. Yet, neither the visual nor the physical aspects puzzle us. We want to learn about those qualities and limitations which we cannot see directly and which become evident only indirectly. God is notorious for his lack of visibility and his preference for disclosing himself only in symbolic acts or words. This habit of his is not as strange as it might at first appear. The major difficulty in understanding either God or man lies in the problem of **how to discover what we cannot immediately see.**

In any age God can easily be overlooked by those who will not put out the effort to discern his presence. In just the same way we remain unknown to ourselves and ignorant of our friends to the extent that we will not move beyond a simple visual and tactile apprehension. We must look for God's qualities in the way he chooses to evidence them in our age. And we uncover these in the same way we come to understand the inner life of a friend—if we care enough to search. We must first discover what around us might disclose God, and we also need to know where it is useless to look, because he has chosen not to appear in that place in that way in that time. **If we can establish a sense of direction, we can build a new knowledge of God in any day.**

Each searcher after God must discover his or her own way. God insists on acting as an individual, and thus he can only be known in an individual way. How each of us will discover him cannot be predicted or settled in advance. On these pages I offer one set of suggestions for your search. My hope is that these ideas can become effective to speed God's discovery in our day. Tomorrow I cannot predict. But it is enough if we learn to find God in our time.

Whenever God is our concern, what has moved men to know him in one age can be successful for revealing him in any other. Of course one route may be more appealing at one time rather than another. A sense of timing is all-important if God is not to be missed. God is neither equally available in every aspect of every day, nor is he absent in the same way in each time. Whoever loses a sensitivity to the peculiar qualities of the hour in which he or she lives will cut himself or herself off from God. At least access to God will be more difficult than it need be if we assume a once successful approach will automatically work in a later time.

Each of us who is interested in God, I propose, should examine those experiences we have all heard reported which, when properly approached, may open an entry way to God. Wherever we encounter these situations, we may meet God—that is, we may if we succeed in building a picture of his powers. Our sketch will be incomplete and insubstantial, however, if we do not at the same time become aware of God's limitations. What are the situations in which God is not able to take part or appear? Or rather, where has he set a limit on his powers when he might act but has agreed not to?

Even if the steps outlined below are changed slightly by each individual reader, they still offer this hope: God can be found in a process of exploration and construction like the one I am asking you to follow here. But we must always remember a major assumption: God appears to each individual as full and real only if we discover *both* his limitations and his powers. He cannot be approached by one idea alone but only by a succession of positive and negative steps.

It would be simpler if only one path or concept led us to or away from God no matter when we were to take up the search. Unfortunately, there is little evidence that God designed either himself or us or his world on the simplest principle possible. Thus, the task we face is complex, and success in discovering God at one time in the past does not guarantee a means of discovery at another time for anyone else. However, we can be encouraged by past reports of finding God. The task he has set us is obviously difficult, but evidently it is not impossible.

GOD IS . . .

I. GOD IS . . .

ABLE TO SUFFER

We men and women are all too often destroyed by suffering. Thus we fear it. No one in a healthy state of mind enjoys pain. It cripples our powers and limits our action. In spite of this, we also know that it is not possible to understand ourselves fully until suffering strips us of self-delusion. The pain we dislike tests our powers of endurance and response in a way that happiness never can. As long as we are in a healthy state of mind, we do not want suffering; we avoid it when we can. Still, to share in another person's suffering, or to have him or her share ours, strengthens friendship. In distress, more intimate knowledge is possible than in easy daily intercourse.

Theologians have denied that God can suffer. To assert God's involvement with pain affronts an exalted notion of his majesty. God should be protected and prohibited from pain because it would tarnish his dignity, some argue. Since we know that suffering changes us, it might change God's nature too if he were able to suffer. However, all suffering is not due to a lack of strength, and God may be like man in this respect. Whoever voluntarily enters into our suffering gives evidence of his power, because he is offering himself to us when he does not have to. Thus, if we discover God in suffering, or at least acknowledge that he is able to suffer, we affirm that he is able to give himself to others voluntarily. Sometimes we human beings want to offer ourselves to others in this way, but we cannot. Thus, if God can enter suffering voluntarily, he is more powerful than we men and women.

When we witness suffering, we are never seeing God

directly. Even if we accept the Christian claim that God suffered in Jesus' crucifixion, it is a man we see on the cross and not God himself. God's ability to give himself freely in time of need can never be manifest directly, as the jeering crowd around the base of Jesus' cross testifies. However, whenever some human being enters into suffering voluntarily in order to relieve our pain or our weakness, in that action we see what God is like.

We may not immediately recognize God in this act, but insight often comes to us later. First we must decide that God is able to suffer. Then, in a human act of sharing suffering, we may finally understand what God is like. Whatever God's capabilities are, he does not suddenly acquire new ones. We may miss discovering him in these self-giving acts if we do not understand what he is able to do. Of course, suffering often changes our nature, and when it does, our eyes may be opened to see what could not be disclosed to us before.

Certainly there is nothing automatic, either about God's presence in suffering or about his decision to enter into it. It would be too easy if we knew that he would always share in our suffering and must always be present in our troubles. But if our friends cannot be counted on for automatic assistance and participation, why should we expect God to come to our rescue automatically? All we learn about God is that he is *able to* share in suffering, not that he must. Perhaps we often miss finding God just because we want to control and prescribe his behavior. But isn't it an evidence of greater power if one can intervene but is not required to do so in every instance? We understand that God may, not that he must, share in suffering and give himself to others. Thus, when his presence comes to us in this way, it has the aspect of a surprise, of a revelation.

Observe the events involved in the passion story as the New Testament records them. What Jesus' disciples understood least was the aspect of suffering involved, and this blocked their ability to visualize God in Christ. As long as Jesus evidenced his power by miracles, it was easy for his followers to accept him as a divine figure, as a Messiah. But when the tables are turned and Jesus stands meekly before Pilate, his once devoted friends are confused and divided. They cannot understand either how divinity can allow suffering or how he can fail to use his divine power to overcome it immediately.

Seeing Jesus suffer, they feel sorry. Yet it is hard to say whether they are more sorry for him or for the disappointment of their own hopes. The recovery of their hope, and the beginning of Christianity, comes with the resurrection act. Christianity means the realization that God can enter into suffering, that he does so freely, not out of necessity. His power is not immediately visible. He can appear to be just as powerless as any human being. He submits, but still he overcomes that death toward which suffering leads us all—or so those who become Christians believe.

II. GOD IS . . .

ABLE TO LOVE

The waiting rooms of psychiatrists are filled with people who cannot love, or at least who cannot give love freely. Some individuals no longer even feel the desire to love. Among those whose desire is still strong, many are frustrated by their inability to love fully and freely. Except for those whose emotions are blocked, all of us can give love sometimes and to some degree. Pain comes to us because our love is often expressed "too little and too late." What we would like to be able to do is to express affection when it is needed and the way we would like to offer it. Rare, and also happy, is the person who can convey his love whenever he wishes, to the person he cares for, in the degree intended, and in a way which can be understood.

We have all found ourselves singled out as objects of attention simply because someone wants something from us. To achieve mutual satisfaction of desire is not a bad human trait. On this ground some of our closest relationships are built. The situation of satisfying a double need turns sour only when someone wants affection from us solely to satisfy his own desire. Either he gives nothing in return or else he offers a false affection, one which is not genuine but simply a mask for emotional greed. We are not satisfied for long if we receive merely an artificial pretense of genuine concern. But beyond the joy of mutual sharing, we yearn to achieve a level of existence which enables us to commit ourselves without becoming entangled in self-centered desire. We would like to be able to give affection simply because someone else needs love. And we wish for the power to do this in a way that does not bind the recipient to a forced expression of gratitude.

Sometimes we find that we are able to convey affection freely and fully, all the while still retaining control of our emotions. Wherever love frees us and does not drain us dry, we meet God. More than that, whenever we receive affection without an accompanying obligation being imposed upon us, we witness God's power at its fullest and its best. But seldom do we escape our own needs and succeed in acting generously without creating a reciprocal demand.

Whatever God's needs are—and his ability to love would imply that he has some—his actions are never totally dominated by his desires in the way base human emotions are. He can and does move independently of his own needs. He can convey love without attracting attention to himself. We often would like to do this, but are only sometimes able to do so. God may be the only really disinterested lover in the world. That is proof enough of his divinity. This is especially true if his disinterest reflects, not listlessness and coldness, but the power of emotional self-control and outer-directed compassion.

All love affairs are complex relationships, even when they are satisfying. This is because our own needs inevitably become entangled with those of the persons we love. Even when our impulse to love carries us so far out that we begin to consider the one we love ahead of ourselves, the success of such a relationship depends on our ability to match and to coordinate two sets of needs and desires. We experience the divine life, then, whenever we discover that God is able to love without involving us in his own internal desire. Where God is present, our relationship need not become tangled in explosive emotions, as so often happens between human beings. To feel love freely and fully expressed—a love which seeks another's and not its own fulfillment—this is to meet God in action. He is found in the form of love which men seek but rarely find.

At the end of a Zazen session in Kyoto, an American girl

reported to the assembled Zen students that she had trouble offering her love. The Zen roshi snapped back: "That is the trouble with you Christians. You always think you *have to* love someone." The point he wanted to make was that the aim of Zen is to train you to rise above, to empty yourself of, the tangled emotions of love. The disinterest which Meister Eckhart discovers at the center of God is more like this state which Zen seeks than is passion.

However, the basic issue is whether disinterest and love can ever be compatible. The ordinary love one human being offers to another is far from disinterested. It wants what it wants when it wants it. By contrast, we discover God whenever we meet disinterested love, that is, a love communicated freely and without self-attachment. To experience that is to locate God. The question is: Can human love be reformed if we work toward that model? Or, is it only by relationship to God that we can achieve that state?

III. GOD IS . . .

ABLE TO BE FREE

Those whose education encourages self-liberation respond by seeking new areas in which to exercise their powers. Not all people learn to extend their freedom in this way. They understand neither themselves nor the world well enough to discover what avenues are and are not open to them. Change becomes possible only when one knows he can and wants to live other than in his present state of inferior development. Thus, it takes strength and intelligence to achieve liberation.

One is not born free. Usually, one lives in the condition one is born to and does not become self-conscious about freedom until one achieves maturity. In fact, maturity can be defined as gaining the knowledge of both one's potential and one's limitations. To become adult is to accept the task of achieving liberation and releasing your powers from artificial restraint. God enters into this struggle too.

God has the intelligence and power necessary to sustain his freedom. And he differs from man in having always possessed full self-awareness, rather than acquiring it gradually as we do. Still, where his relations with the human race are concerned, God also must strive to achieve full freedom. He cannot relate freely to one who is not free. A free person cannot be comrade with a slave. To share the human condition is to share limited freedom, or at least the limited degree to which most men have developed their inborn powers. A fully free being, whether God or man, desires that others be free in the same way. Only those who are partially free and partially bound envy freedom and conspire to inhibit the potential of others. The power of genuine freedom is the ability to free others in relationship to you.

In this sense, God's full freedom would be empty if it were simply an expression of his unrestrained power. For example, due to his power he could determine every event in advance, but his freedom also allows him not to do so. To be meaningful, our freedom must be involved in the life of someone else. God committed himself to man's struggle for liberation from the moment he gave the signal "go" for the creation of our world. When we meet God, we do not encounter simply another blind power struggle. We discover someone who possesses the power to be free himself and yet to control us, but who nevertheless accepts our freedom in relation to his own.

Others, those whose freedom is threatened and precarious, are afraid of every action they do not control. A weak man is comfortable only when he can hold other persons within the boundaries of an imposed code. Some of us would turn God into a source of comfort by convincing ourselves that his nature is characterized by necessary boundaries and that that is the way God should be. To face a free God is an overwhelming experience for anyone not confident of his or her own power to sustain free action. Even theologians—whose business it is to talk about and to God—often flee from this unsettling confrontation with open-ended divine freedom. They plead instead for a necessary God.

Whenever we meet someone who is able to let others relate freely to him, we know he or she does not feel threatened but instead encourages others to be free in their own expressions. We also experience an important aspect of God's nature. Such freedom does not mean capricious or irrational behavior. It includes the ability to act on the basis of what one thinks and plans, as well as the capacity to develop our own human potential into an effective instrument. It is necessary to achieve such control if we want to create anything novel or new.

One who is fully free can explore what might be as well

as what is. There can be only one God, but many beings may share freedom. To meet God is to realize that we are encouraged to work for freedom by one who is not jealous simply to preserve his own uniqueness. He can and will share with us what characteristically is his own. That is, we can achieve equality with the divine if we are ready to follow his lead and shape our own course of action decisively.

The present struggle of minorities and Third World peoples represents the greatest press for freedom in human history, at least since last century's push against monarchies and empires. The black experience in America illustrates the power which religion has to survive slavery, and also the strength it can add to the drive for liberation. In spite of oppression, many Black Christians stayed close to traditional Christianity and did not suffer "the death of God" with liberal Protestants.

Prison literature has established a powerful tradition beginning with Paul, but the depth of spiritual literature which prisons can produce cannot be used as an argument for perpetuating slave conditions. A life of ease subdues man's press for freedom, while the search for liberation sustains religion. In this struggle, and not in rest, God can be located. However, God's nature does not allow either him or us an easy freedom. Freedom involves a constant pressure to remain open and to control the powers that would enslave us all, God included. God succeeds in his drive to remain free. We men and women walk along God's path when we succeed in sustaining our openness too.

IV. GOD IS . . .

ABLE TO CONTROL

There are moments when all human beings go out of control. And there are times when the world no longer seems to respond to anyone's guidance. There are also occasions when we are able to keep ourselves in check and direct events. We admire this ability to exercise definitive control, whether it is exhibited physically in athletics, exemplified religiously in spirituality, or manifested politically in public affairs.

Whenever we encounter a power of control that is capable of giving life to new human or natural potentialities, we learn about God by virtue of what he is able to do. As men and women, we fight constantly to sustain our control over events, because any successful control formula seldom works as well in new situations. Our power tends to ebb if not continually reinforced by our will. God is exceptional (i.e., divine), because he maintains control without being concerned to renew his effort constantly.

God is not only able to enforce control in order to sustain his present action, he is able to extend his hold out into the future to assure that his aim is accomplished. What is past appears to him as if it were the live present now going on. If as human beings we look at the past as it extends forward, we can recognize what God's power of control means. He can hold himself to any path he has elected. He does not reject his own past, as we often do if it is full of mistakes. He accepts what his actions have produced, whereas we men and women often spend our time running away from our past decisions. Accepting past mistakes insures the future, if our control is sufficient to make the needed changes.

However, we encounter God's ability to control the future only in the form of a promise. If we accept the divine promise, this means that we sustain our confidence in his future and acknowledge his ability to constitute our world as it is now and as we meant it to be. It also means that we recognize how he sustains his own past. God's capacity to control the present is the same thing as his power to refrain from total dominance. This is God's offer to share control. Direction that deserves the name divine is not offered on an all-or-nothing basis. God has the power to stay loose.

Those uncertain of their ability offer the greatest resistance to any request to share control. Such men and women prefer to coerce the future by attempting to determine everything open to their influence. When we meet someone who allows the future to remain open, we uncover an image of God. God is able to impose necessity, but he abides by contingency or uncertainty. He is able to overpower everything that lies in his way, but he restrains this ability for total control to permit others to exercise their directional energies.

God can make the future into a mirror image of the past, but he restricts his power and accepts uncertainty with its resulting incompleteness of knowledge. Only those who are trying to be God picture God as eternally possessing certain knowledge of all events. God's control is so powerful that he does not need to coerce everything and everyone in order to prove himself. He can afford the luxury of being underestimated and misunderstood.

His willingness to restrict his power in order to share control with us evidences his ability to assume command at a time of his own choosing. Considered abstractly, we do not know when or even whether God may want to exercise this ability to intervene. Nevertheless, his capacity for control extends to the total reconstruction of events and peoples and worlds. What he concedes to other sources of control for an indefinite time, that he can also reclaim and reconstitute. When we discover a power so self-confident that it need not press to determine every event, we have met a God of relaxed command. This divinity is one who can release his control and leave options open to us just because he is secure in his abilities and sure of his power.

Aristotle, Augustine, Calvin, and a host of traditionalists have all wanted God to determine the future with absolute fixity in order to stem the panic we humans feel when we face constant uncertainty. Due to our uneven ability to hold things steady, God understands why we might want him to determine events once and for all, but he refuses to be stampeded by human anxiety. He can open the valve on human contingency and freedom as far as he likes. He can even allow a certain leeway in the processes of nature, and still he does not have to worry about his ability either to maintain or to regain control when he chooses.

Human beings are certainly unlike God when they scurry about constantly protecting their possessions. God laughs a little when he hears Jesus tell us to "Consider the lilies of the field; they toil not neither do they spin." He knows that this is a God-like attitude, and that few men will be able to calm themselves down far enough to follow Jesus' advice. To rest like a lily, to grow like a lily without concern, is an image that reveals God's attitude, not man's. But then, Jesus' words tell us as much or more about God than they do about man. Our own insecurities we know all too well. It is God's life, and our ability to relate to it, that arouses our curiosity.

V. GOD IS . . .

ABLE TO BE PRESENT WITH US

Quite often people complain that God is either distant or withdrawn or hidden. (Of course, there are those who find him obvious, too.) Probably on most occasions God does not intrude himself but stays patiently out of sight. Upon reflection, we may agree that this is not such a bad characteristic. However, it would be more comfortable for religious men and women if they could always be sure of God's presence. But if we put aside our selfish desire to have God available on demand, we realize that the important divine ability is his power to be present when he wants to be. Most of us lack this quality. At crucial moments we are sometimes unable to make ourselves available to others just when we most want to.

More than physical presence—which is a relatively simple matter—we human beings find it hard to reveal our attitudes, our emotions, and our wishes with the clarity we would like. When we try to make ourselves known to someone, we often do not succeed. To open ourselves fully to another human being requires us to empty ourselves of our concerns and preoccupations in order to become at one with another in his or her life.

To become the other qua other is our most difficult task. But whenever we see this accomplished, we recognize a divine power at work. God is sometimes pictured as being so powerful that his immediate presence would either destroy or overwhelm us. The truth is that he is able to set his power aside and become one with us without threatening our independence. Jesus' phrase, "blessed are the humble in spirit," is amazingly applicable to God.

29

Even when we are able to place ourselves fully beside another human being, the effect is often coercive. The person feels under pressure to be like us, although we may deny that is our intention. Even if we do not intend it, any exercise of superior power naturally creates, not a situation of equality, but one of condescension on our part. God's unique ability lies in being able to become present to us without imposing coercion. But for just this reason, many of us remain unaware of the divine availability.

If we consider God's presence in Jesus, we know it must have been noncoercive, because men are still divided over how to respond to Jesus. This uncertainty began during his life and continues still. If God exuded unlimited power, his presence would always force a consistent response from us. Instead, Jesus' appearance among men was so noncoercive that we are still mystified over how God could have been present in Jesus and still not have controlled our reaction to Jesus' appearance. Evidently, divinity does not need the uniformity of response we human prima donnas often demand.

Instead of destroying us or even coercing our response, to feel God's presence has the unusual effect of setting us free. If we feel free, it must be because God is able to make himself available to us on our terms rather than on his. This is an amazing ability, since his power would allow him to dictate any conditions he chose. Our presence with another human being, however pleasant and comforting, has the effect of constraint. It simply forces him or her to bend toward us and our ways, no matter how innocent our intent. It is the essence of divinity to be available to us and yet increase our freedom at the same time. God adds to our sense of release as few persons do, because we realize he seeks only to control himself and not others. To meet a noncoercive presence whose effect is to stimulate us to seek our own independence, this is to discover God in an unforgettable moment. No human being can have quite the same effect on us.

"Let it be, let it be" advises the verse of the Beatles' song. We like to listen to words like that. In fact, ours is an age caught up and absorbed in a world of strong sound not quite of a human dimension. We cannot let it be; only God can. We create and we want to control our creations. It takes power and an infinite self-assurance to release what we have made or once enjoyed. This is what prayer is all about, or what it should aim to achieve. In our natural state, we leave neither ourselves nor others nor nature nor God alone. We need to pray a lot if we want to be strengthened enough to "let it be."

Our human powers are considerable, but we know they still fall short of absolute control. To have our prayers answered means to find ourselves able to release our control and to trust rather than to despair. To feel the presence of such a power of self-control is to find ourselves in God's hands. He can let us be, whereas we constantly beseech and besiege both him and others to yield to our demands. "He's got the whole world in his hands," says the Negro spiritual. That is neither an obvious fact nor is it easy for frail humans to accept. When we do manage to accept and relax, we know God's power has come up behind our own.

VI. GOD IS . . .

ABLE TO USE FORCE

If we paint God as docile, we will never meet him as an individual. We might be more comfortable with a tame God, but the violence of the world stands unexplained unless God commands at least as much force as we observe around us. Actually, he must have enough power at his disposal to exceed the terror and coercion we witness in action around us. It takes force to control force. The powers loose in nature and in man are subject to no final restraint unless God can match and control these with his own legions. We need not always see or feel God's force, but he must be able to unleash it at will. If not, we will all finally be crushed between the world's contesting powers.

Any use of force always involves some destruction; therefore, God must be able to absorb into his nature such loss as the possession and use of power entails. He is not so timid as to refrain from using the force at his disposal simply because some destruction is involved. However, if his power is constructive as well as destructive, he turns force loose to destroy in such a way that nature and humanity still survive. If force can annihilate, it can also revive life. To use power amateurishly means to be unable to reverse its destructive side effects. Perhaps we see God's divinity whenever force visits us with destructive power and yet life survives or is even revived in the process.

Perhaps men and women cannot remain creative very long unless they feel force applied from time to time. Our human tendency is to close ourselves off and shut ourselves up, in much the same way that business corporations and political societies turn rigid and stagnant in due time. In this case, only force can blast open what has become closed, although such energy cannot be unleashed without effecting some destruction as a side effect.

However, if force is unleashed with accompanying control, the loss of present structures, which at the time seems like death to societies and to people, may become a prelude to new life. Force can create new forms of life as well as destroy, provided its use is divine in its control and is not in fumbling hands. To feel the impact of force, to be undone by it, to survive, and to find greater vitality released—this surely is to experience God's ability to use power creatively.

If we experience a violent force rampaging blindly or without regard, we speak of the destruction in its wake as tragic, as a loss which is to no avail, as "the work of the Devil." All applied force comes so close to demonic destruction that many want to paint God as a pacifist in order to keep him clear of such involvement. Just because power is often destructive and clumsily controlled, we associate force with loss. Nevertheless, hard pressure is needed before we can create anything new. The person who has not been bent by force cannot have learned God's depths from the struggle to survive. God is present when power is used, but only if both control and survival are the aim of the pressure unleashed.

In *The Saviors of God* Kazantzakis depicts God as needing help from men. God struggles constantly, as Kazantzakis portrays him. The force involved in this clash is often painful and bloody, although sometimes it can be ecstatic and rewarding. God may demand assistance from men as he struggles with himself, but the issue is: Does he do this because he has to or because he wants to? In *Zorba the Greek*, we sense that God loves the earth and its human pleasures. In *Saint Francis*, Kazantzakis depicts the struggle necessary if man is to be converted away from his attachment to luxury and achieve spirituality.

All this toil and agony is a part of God's life. It is also the

33

only avenue to human insight. God sometimes is gentle with us, but not often. Ironically, a kindly priest or a gentle mother reveals very little about God's use of force, comforting as both figures may be. He created power; his life is based on force; he uses and controls it. To discover God, however, is to read Kazantzakis' portrayal of the struggle to subdue destruction, then to accept it, only to find that the earth is still alive and life has been preserved after the storm has passed. "And the bush was not consumed."

VII. GOD IS . . .

ABLE TO UNDERSTAND

We all want to increase our human understanding. The problem we face is not so much that the
world either is opaque or exceeds our grasp. It is that we
often lose our power of self-control, and increasing
understanding depends on our keeping a steady grasp.
Whenever we are able to comprehend with ease and
without interference, we intersect the line which God's
knowledge follows. The difference between God and man
is not that God is omniscient, as he is so often pictured. In
order to be God, he does not need to hold every fact about
the world continually in his sight. He does need to be able
to marshall his understanding with ease and in such a
manner that it never slips away. God can afford to be
patient about the future. He does not need to demand the
final resolution of all events in advance. However, his
ability to fathom events fully as they arrive and never to
lose his control marks the quality of his understanding as
divine.

Few, if any, of us claim complete self-understanding.
Self-clarity of this depth may lie beyond human grasp. Or,
if moments of full disclosure do come to us, we do not
seem able to sustain them long. Rather, the rare moments
of lucidity we do achieve must be held over in memory to
be enjoyed. God is unique in being able continuously to
sustain full self-understanding, even though this su-
perawareness needs constantly to be adjusted to the
changing course of events instituted by free men.

God's mind meets each novelty with instantaneous
realignment. Whenever you find clear, sustained self-

understanding held in firm relation to the acts of others, you have met God—whether you realize it or not. Of course, God also understands the events of the physical world and their evolutions perfectly. Freedom and decision are not involved in following the course of the stars, once they are fixed in orbit and the laws governing them are set. Thus, God's understanding of the natural order is not as difficult as his self-understanding or his understanding of why men and women act as they do. Both divine and human nature involve a freedom difficult to control. Men and women try for freedom; God achieves it through self-understanding and control.

If we have trouble understanding ourselves, comprehending others is even more difficult. In the first place, if full self-comprehension is required as a condition for clear understanding of others, our vision will remain clouded, or at least it will be incomplete. Beyond that, however, lies another difficulty: we often interpret others from our perspective rather than theirs. Therefore, our goal should be to set aside our own categories and experiences in order to understand others just as they are, on terms appropriate to them rather than us. We often settle for interpretations of the actions of others which mirror our self-interpretations. We discover how God understands on any occasion when we are able to set interpretive schemes aside and fully understand someone just as he or she is.

Such power and clarity of understanding—one so calmly disciplined that self-images are set aside and another person is known simply as he is—this is a divine prerogative. In our own lives we may find that we understand ourselves in the midst of a struggle to understand someone else, and in a sense, God understands himself more fully when he comes to know us as our human lives develop freely. But for him this is not a disclosure of hidden parts. That is, he does not need to struggle with himself before he can understand us, nor does he mirror himself in the life of another as we seem to do. Where the ability to understand can be sustained, and where another is known in and for him or herself without self-involvement, there God can be met. Human understanding is seldom able to complete its task, but God is recognizable by just that ability.

In his *Ethics*, Spinoza claims that all of our individual minds are, in varying degrees, part of the divine mind. Thus, we do not have far to go to see ourselves and our world as God sees both himself and others, that is, fully and clearly. The problem with Spinoza's theory is that our minds simply do not feel in communion with divine insight, even allowing for Spinoza's admission that our minds need improvement before we can expect to exercise such divine understanding. Of course, we sometimes sense a divine power of insight when we are in the presence of a few men.

However, even if we succeed in achieving our goal of universal education, we have largely abandoned the hope that very many can be sustained for very long at a high level of insight. Besides, to know the good does not always result in doing the good. Therefore many destructive minds achieve a powerful level of insight too. We have just lived through a human holocast which came on us even after we had brought a portion of humanity to enlightenment in the modern age. Thus, we stand amazed before God's depth of understanding, but even more before his ability both to sustain it and to employ it constructively. We human beings seem to do this only rarely. We can raise a few to this level, but not enough for long enough to overcome our limitations as a race.

VIII. GOD IS . . .

ABLE TO CREATE

We celebrate our talent to create, whether in art or in science, and we enjoy the visible results of such power. But those who find themselves able to create are also plagued by pain. This agony blocks out the joy we feel over what we are able to bring to birth. We are proud of all that mankind has learned to do, but the unpublished human story is one of vast talent wasted by impotency. The sad tale which we tend to suppress is of human creative powers stopped in midcourse and thus denied fruition, whether by internal or by external opposition. Thus, surveying humanity as a whole, we are more aware of our inability to create than our power to give life to new forms. The few magnificent exceptions, which are dramatically publicized, do not paint either a realistic or balanced picture of the waste involved in the human struggle. We prefer to celebrate the accomplishments of human culture. Therefore, when we see in God the power to create new forms of life, this is an activity more rare in human affairs than we like to admit.

Human creative ability at times flowers magnificently. When it pours forth, it seems almost inexhaustible. And this is one reason its unknown depths terrify those who would but cannot create novel art forms or new theories. A genius is haunted because he or she is not sure that his creative capacity can be sustained for very long. It is better to be born without the ability to create than to possess a talent and be unable to carry out its promise. Men and women are tortured more by what they might do but cannot than by what they actually accomplish. Thus, if we discover that God encounters no internal impediment in exercising his creative expression, we locate in him such self-fulfilled power as men only dream of. We establish a model for God's uninhibited life if we outline those conditions which set the creative person apart from others. First, all self-concern must be lost. If a person's attention constantly swings back to his or her creative personality, the risk is that talent will simply spin around in self-absorption instead of being given a definite form outside the person. Somehow we need to lose the fear we have of experiencing our creative powers. Rather than cringing in anticipation of adverse judgment on our attempts at new expressions, we should work for what we want to express and center our attention beyond our own ego. We need to concentrate on what might be and not paralyze ourselves by fear of failure.

God, then, is one who is able to externalize his creative powers freely. Thus, whenever we encounter such spontaneous behavior, we understand God better. We can use this experience to form our image of God's ability to create, but we can also use it as our own model too. Nothing blocks God's self-expression except his concern not to destroy what already has existence. Of course, this principle of nondestruction is not perfectly embodied in the world, since many of the forms we create compete and so destroy each other.

The constant presence of conflict in the world testifies to the depths of God's limitless creative capacities and to the clash he faces when he makes any decision. But evidently God decided to allow destructive competition into the world order he elected. To know God is to understand his unopposed ability to create new forms of life outside himself however he chooses. That is, God creates without the conflict of internal inhibitions. On the other hand, fighting ourselves is a primary human occupation.

In a poem entitled "An Island in the Moon," William Blake laments the agony of anyone who is talented enough to create but who cannot bring forth.

> To be or not to be
> Of great capacity

We often romanticize our human powers. We talk lightly as if creation were an easy matter. In point of fact, our unused talent often destroys us from the inside because we are painfully aware of what we could have done but have not done. We feel that all the world will be our judge if we fail, and we know we may lose if we try to create something new. So acting in fear, we attempt to conserve our power by burying our allotted talent in the ground, just as Jesus depicts in one of his parables. Yet once an artist or writer or craftsman hits his pace and finds a mold into which he can release his latent talent, new productions pour forth and any adverse judgment seems insignificant. But few of us make it to that near-divine status. The majority of us cringe in fear of our ability and our power—or else we bemoan our lack of it.

IX. GOD IS . . .

ABLE TO WORSHIP

Worship is a special function, and many are neither suited for it nor should they expect to be able to enter into it. Yet, if we pay attention only to our automatic human abilities, we either will never find God or else will uncover only a rather bland image. We are much more likely to discover God in unusual and difficult human activities and capacities, although this is true only if we are willing to go beyond our inhibitions to explore eccentricity. To worship means to admit that we are inferior to a greater power, even if we think we possess magnificent abilities. To enter into worship we must humble ourselves and draw strength from giving thanks. To evidence appreciation genuinely in prayer means to admit that we depend on another for the power or assistance we receive.

Not all of us can accept such a posture, and so the ability to worship freely remains rare. All who go to churches are not worshiping. When we can place ourselves in such an attitude, the resulting experience is decisive in our quest of the divine. If we fail to worship we will miss at least one important face of God. Anyone who cannot learn what worship means, who cannot feel the human need it serves, is blocked from realizing God's presence. However, difficult as it is to achieve a state of worship, what is strange to discover is that God is able to worship too. To say this only seems odd because God is usually thought to be the object of all worship. Thus, we seem to be forced to say that God worships himself. In a certain sense this is true, in that God draws strength from giving thanks, yet all the while he is the source of strength. His thankfulness is

41

for his own nature and its creative powers. However, occasionally he gives thanks for the assistance rendered by men and women toward completing his projects.

We find God through worship only if we discover him as he worships beside us. Many of us miss God in services of formal worship, in the recital of liturgy, and in the performance of ritual. This is because we expect to find God as the main object of attention, the receiver of our thanks. Of course, in a formal sense he is. But we will miss the inner vitality of God if we do not understand that he is just as able to give praise and thanks as he is to receive it.

God can sit beside us and be silent while he and we are deep in prayer. As human beings we tend to be grudging. We hoard any praise given to us. God has the refreshing freedom and ability to turn praise around and join us in giving thanks. To be able to unbend, to offer himself to another freely and without restraint—that is God's secret source of strength. However, the first time we try this, we may feel increased vulnerability rather than strength. God can offer himself in all genuine humility, because he is not afraid of ridicule as we are.

In order to give thanks ungrudgingly, we must be able to surrender any position of superiority. Odd as it may seem, God discovers strength from confessing his sins in just the way we do. He has directed men and nature down a difficult road, due to the less than optimal decisions he made at the moment of creation. He needs to say thanks for those who continue, in spite of his questionable choice of a fallible world, to follow him in trust. God's sins are not ours, but he has on his shoulders the burden for allowing negative aspects into the world he chose to create. We worship because we need strength to face that world. God worships in order to pray for our strength in the face of the adversities he freely created and placed in our way. He draws strength from his ability to yield himself in worship. Thus, we discover God in worship when we understand how and why he wants to join us in prayer.

Jesus' use of prayer provides a model for us. He did not retire from the world to pray. He was arrested and then killed while in the midst of praying. Jesus derided long, formal, self-righteous prayers on the grounds that God already knows us better than we know ourselves. In fact, God may know more than he cares to know about us! Jesus did pray and worship on occasion. However, he did so in such a simple way that it should lead us to suspect that men really do not have to go far to reach God, if only we can find the way.

The whole meaning of the Christian doctrine of the incarnation, after all, is to assert that God has joined us. If this biblical report is true, God should be able to join us in worship. Too often our churchly forms of worship appear to be a concerted effort to raise ourselves up to God. The truth is that God joins us quietly and often without our recognizing him. We need not spend hours in agonized prayer if only we could recognize God's presence when he is beside us.

X. GOD IS . . .

ABLE TO HEAL

The human body has an ability to restore itself, but this power has certain limitations. The body's resilience gradually decreases over the years, and some attacks upon it are destructive beyond any medical ability to repair. The same is true, of course, of both our psychic and our spiritual lives. People sustain wounds in their daily intercourse from the battles they are drawn into, and many never recover. We can repair some damage to our psyche and spirit, even though in certain cases the road to health is long and difficult. If it were not for this self-regenerative power, we would be constant cripples both in body and in spirit. Yet we know we cannot ward off permanent destruction forever.

Physicians come to us in all types and sizes. Healing comes to us from without as well as from within, through our natural powers of renewal. When we freely acknowledge that the instrument which heals us comes from beyond ourselves, we are in that special situation in which God can be known. God heals himself. And he needs to, for he keeps himself open to all the wounds we constantly inflict upon ourselves and others. Yet, he is not content, as we might be, simply to restore himself.

He continually offers healing to others. He also offers us the ability to restore ourselves, and he does so without regard for the merit or the lack of it in our particular struggle. If healing comes to us through an instrument which makes no demand for reward, this experience of healing is the context within which the recognition of God can take place.

able to heal

The difficulty is that such healing, at least as we experience it now, is at best partial and always subject to repeated loss. Moreover, some of God's promised healing is postponed to that unspecified future time when all destructive tendencies in the world will be brought to a halt. Our present experience in religion is more the realization that healing has been promised to us, rather than that our health is completely and permanently restored.

To heal means to control what destroys and to provide the power to reverse its damage. We experience some healing at present simply due to the promise of future restoration. Thus, the accomplishment of future healing depends on our belief that God's control is sufficient to subdue all the powers that destroy. Faith means that we who suffer trust the eventual capability of the one who promises to heal us and to restore all damage.

To believe in the power of God to heal our psychic and spiritual wounds is to trust in God. And at the same time we discover him in this act. Since the promise of a future action is involved, a God who would do this cannot be fully and finally uncovered in any present event. Therefore, to believe in God's power to restore what has been damaged is to know him as future-oriented and as only partly known to us now. Most of the destruction we witness daily all around us remains unrepaired. Sometimes we are able to effect new life and health through our own efforts. But we will never find God if we look for him only in our present experience.

The key to discovering the core of God's being is the realization of his power to control the future. Yet, the center of God's nature is never fully open for our inspection. Even in his own life, he lives more in the future than either the past or present. After all, healing is pointless if it is not accomplished with the future in mind. Only the sick in spirit are interested merely in setting past injuries straight. One who is well can forgive another just because his own energies move in a different direction from an obsession over the wrongs of the past. To come alive again means to recover a future-orientation—and perhaps to find God, because both of us are moving in the same direction.

A medical doctor is one who is engaged in a life of healing. This science has advanced in power beyond any dream primitive man had of controlling his health. Yet today every doctor still feels the limitations of his healing powers no less than before. Modern medicine can extend life, but no doctor can either reverse death or guarantee that the life he restores will be pleasant. If we survey the array of instruments and technology today's doctor can employ, we realize the powers at his disposal, but we also discover the limitations beyond which neither he nor we can go.

Ministers of religion and psychological counselors practice healing, but the number of people still locked within themselves or within asylums testify to our inability to cure all men at once in body and mind. We can neither reverse the past nor escape the present, but doesn't healing really mean to open a new future for man? To discover a physician who can do that for us is to find an instrument through whom God stoops down to earth to heal. As a healer, he is the God of our future.

XI. GOD IS . . .

ABLE TO RISK REJECTION

We frail human beings spend a great deal of time trying to prevent our being rejected. Ironically, God controls rejection perfectly. Thus, he can control acceptance easily. The course of development of our world and every action in it could have been fully preprogrammed. Had God done this, he could have insured his own worship and praise. God is a gambler, however. Since he invented the laws of chance, God need not insist on maintaining strict control over men. Because he can stand to experience suffering, he is able to humble himself. But of course, in setting aside his power and even his own interest, he risks the possible rejection which freedom always involves.

God could have decided to remove all chance and human decision in the shaping of events. Then, all events would be based on natural causes. Our world would be simply the fixed result of necessity, a neat arrangement that would please many. God and men both enjoy thinking along those lines, and in our minds we construct necessary worlds. In point of fact though, God seems to have preferred the chances involved in contingency. He is pleased to accept the risk of our rejection which living with uncertainty involves. We recognize this fact about God only when we first accept the way we respond to the world naturally, and then find ourselves turning our innocent reaction into a source of new insight into God.

Why would God do this? Why would he accept contingency when he could impose necessity? Why should God compromise his own interests and even endanger his goals? He has the power to insure control and his own success by clamping down an iron necessity all around us. If our recognition of God is left clouded and uncertain, the danger of rejection involves a risk for God. A system which outlawed contingency and freedom and gave us a clear knowledge about God and his mode of operation—would make a much safer world than the one we have.

Certainty would help us relate to God and accept his ways. Instead, even our vision of God is unclear and subject to change. If we do not see God properly, or with any steady vision, we may turn away from him. On the other hand, many men and women try furiously to reveal themselves fully to others, hoping to gain acceptance and understanding. Children naturally and spontaneously turn outward to others, until they become hurt or sick. Then as they mature, they become more guarded. The young turn inward in self-protection only as age and sophistication creep up on them and dampen their youthful spontaneity.

When we reflect on it, to humble oneself, to even partially relinquish control, to risk rejection—all this can be a show of strength and not weakness. Whenever we feel we are forced into a precarious position, we usually confess our weakness. We would control every event if we could. But we might become confused by the magnitude of the task, and we can't take that chance. Only the truly strong dare to risk bending down to others when they do not have to.

To be gentle and passive, when one could control by force, actually requires great restraint. God's physical power is enormous. His mental ability to control his thoughts, however, is even more phenomenal. Whenever he is gentle, it is not through impotency. It is because of a conscious concern for the effect his action has on those who are more vulnerable to injury.

What perhaps is most phenomenal about divinity is that God is able to shorten his memory. Human recollection is often faulty through our inadequacy. God can instantaneously recall from his memory bank every item in the world's history to date. However, at times he chooses to blot out such remembrance and to remain piously ignorant. It is fortunate for us that God has this ability to forget selectively and that he also chooses to exercise it. Otherwise, it would be hard for him ever to forgive us completely.

We forgive neither ourselves nor others when we refuse to forget. Instead, we constantly pour over the same old issues. As evidence of our weakness, we insist on tying our memory to the past. God is more future-oriented in his thought than we are, but at their best human beings can be future-oriented too. God has the power to remember and hold onto the past. He does so at times, but he prefers a future-orientation and the forgiveness which forgetfulness makes possible. That is, he forgives and forgets when we allow him to relate to us in this way. But first, we have to stop nursing a grudge against the world's unfairness.

In our relation to other human beings, memory is as much a hindrance as a help. We need to recall past experiences; they are the ties that bind us to one another. The child who forgets his parents is worse than ungrateful. God promised Israel he would not forget them as his chosen people. Jews live scattered all over the world but still have the memory of their past relationship to God, and they wait for the promise to be fulfilled. On the other hand, once an unfortunate incident has arisen, we often change from what we once were. Bitter memories block us from easily resuming a former relationship.

To possess a memory is to remind someone of what we know about his past. Often that simply makes him avoid us in the future. We always fear that some preserved memory will return to evict us from the secure life we have built on top of an early folly. Actually, we can risk a haunting memory if we couple it with forgiveness. When we are successful in doing this, we continue to move out from our newly secure position and risk rejection, just as the venturesome young do so easily and naturally. Youth is a matter of being able to accept risk and move on to the future, rather than letting memory stop in the past. God demonstrates his lack of age by his constant risk of rejection for the sake of the future.

XII. GOD IS . . .

ABLE TO LAUGH

When we look back, it is amazing to realize how God's sense of humor has been overlooked by those who have described him, particularly by serious theologians. Of course, God cannot have a careless, an easy, or even a vindictive sense of humor such as ours is at times. However, God has often been described in harsh, cold, and austere images. Even those who see him revealed as loving interpret this as a very serious love. His affection is portrayed melodramatically, with a touch of sadness, rather than as gay or enthusiastic or spontaneous as so much of the love is that we find attractive in human beings. True, the world has enough depressing aspects to give any concerned God enough to weep about. Who would care to know a God who achieved his humor, as some do, by belittling human suffering? We would reject a God who used laughter as a means to shut out the pain both around him and within him.

Nevertheless, the ability to laugh is crucial to those who achieve effective insight into themselves and others. Anyone too intent and too constantly serious is likely to misunderstand both the world and himself. Such people are distrusted by their fellows, because they press down too hard and thus are depressing to be around. A sense of humor requires a lightness of touch and, above all, a sense of perspective. If we lack a balanced perspective, even our understanding becomes "too heavy" and misses its mark by being ponderous.

All too often we are sanctimonious and self-important buffoons. Surely any God who understands himself must laugh at our foolishness at times. Yet, some aspects of human behavior are genuinely funny, and God must respond to such talent just as we do. However, like us, God must be torn between laughter and tears. He is a "Jewish comedian," retaining a touch of humor in spite of his tragic sense of life.

Above all, to find a God who is able to laugh is surely one of our few hopes. Whenever we lose the ability to laugh at ourselves, we know we are close to being trapped in our own mental torture chamber. When this happens, we fall into a psychological pit from which we cannot escape until we learn to laugh again. We find our aid and our release in life's humorous side. We gladly pay millions to laugh. We seek out that most prized of all human talents, the comic, just because it relieves our seriousness.

If our relationship to God were always heavy, joining in religious practices would only indulge our introspective self-intensity. God would then be the most self-defeating being we had ever met, if he could not save us from our obsessive seriousness. To be saved means partly to gain release from a too intense self-concentration. A totally serious God would lock us more deeply inside ourselves, but, if he can meet us with a sense of humor, that releases us from our self-imposed burdens. To know God is to learn to laugh with God, not only to weep.

As a revelation of God, it is true that the New Testament is not a very humorous book. Yet, it is also true that Jesus evidences more self-detachment and less pomposity than the more formally religious men around him or most of those who came after him to control his church. There is a brightness in Jesus' promise and an openness in his attitude toward the future which professional religion often lacks. All of this indicates that God is able to smile more than his priests care to admit.

There is laughter in heaven as well as rage, humor in God's speech as well as moral exhortation. A lightness of touch in self-reflection leads God not to take himself as seriously as we do. After all, he does not have to struggle as intently for self-understanding as men do. God can smile at our frantic efforts and laugh at our foibles and mistakes. Given his power, he can afford error and the humor that rests upon realizing that he is still in control. Every comedian seeks to imitate God and envies the rapt attention with which his earthly audience listens.

Woody Allen is a very funny man, but his humor has a serious touch. In *Getting Even* one chapter is called "My Philosophy." It is a parody on ponderous philosophy and philosophers. "Eternal nothingness is OK if you are dressed for it," he says. He ends with an aphorism I'm sure God would find funny too: "Not only is there no God, but try getting a plumber on the weekend." What the theologian must do is explain the art of the humorist, even if he cannot be one.

Since God had options when he ordered the world, he could have created it dry and humorless. The fact that humor is possible gives us some idea of where the humorist ranks on the divine entertainment scale. God could have kept laughter away and insured himself a serious reception. Priests and ministers would be more comfortable if they could only be sure their seriousness would never be taken lightly. But they are always placed in danger if God can indulge in laughter. Shouldn't humor open up one path to divinity for us—even if its surprise element threatens us all and drives some away?

XIII. GOD IS . . .

ABLE TO APPEAR IN THE DETAIL

"God is in the detail" is a famous remark Mies van der Rohe made about architectural style. Yet it is as illuminating about God and his powers as it is about the beauty of a building's structure. We have all seen poorly executed examples of a basically beautiful style, whether in music, art, or literature. Evidently, genius lies not so much in the overall concept as in the care and precision with which materials and surfaces are brought together. The real master is the one who is in control of subtle detail, and this is as true of slick modern buildings as it is of a baroque chapel or a medieval cathedral. We all know that radical ideas—whether in politics or in art—come easily. Few have the skill, the patience, and the subtlety of mind needed to carry new ideas out with precision and intimacy of detail. It is easy to copy the broad design, difficult to get the master's nuances. God, then, appears more in the detail than in the broad design of the universe.

Thus, we waste our breath—unless we enjoy cocktail party conversation—when we argue for the superiority of one historical period, or one style or art or etiquette, over another. Life can be lived in many ways. Men and women can be dressed and combed in many ways. Religions are possible along many styles. Everything depends on the care taken with detail as to whether the result is crude or admirable. We also waste our breath, then, arguing that we will liberate men or women by changing from one form or style of religion to another, because we can turn any way of life against ourselves and use it repressively rather than creatively. Our dilemma is that the care with which a design or a program is executed is an individual matter of style and talent. Thus, it cannot be designed for mass consumption or programmed so as to be effective in every individual instance. Neither can God work with all of us at once.

Now, if God is in the detail in architecture and in human affairs, he has ironically designed the world so that it is easier to miss him than to find him. A person who either does not care to see, or will not devote the patience to an intricate search, either misses God every time or else settles on some crass and unthinking popular idol. A God who lives in the detail of life or art or religion is always hard to find. Few of us hold still long enough to discern him in subtle places. Of course, the reports of discovering God are many. Successful organized religion is built on an ability to popularize God publicly, to make him appealing to the masses.

Successful priests are gifted with this interpretative ability, a skill in mass producing an experience of God for the many—at least momentarily. This is a necessary art just because God's forms of presence are so subtle that divinity will be overlooked unless professional religion magnifies God's image a thousandfold. Of course, we encounter some inevitable distorted exaggerations in this process. Thus, some of us eventually become disillusioned by popular religious movements when God still seems to elude us in the long, quiet moments no matter how dramatic his appearances are in church.

It is only in the care of the detail in certain experiences, e.g., in the visual arts or in the use of words, that God can really be captured with any lasting result. Learning to do this is an individual affair, and our success can never be easily duplicated for another. As with training in music appreciation, one can be taught to listen and learn how to be aware of detail, but this only prepares us; it does not give us a final grasp.

A God who cares about detail is both more interesting and more personal than a raging God of war or a thundering moralist. If the general rules of life are not as important as the way they are carried out, this leaves us some latitude to worship and to carry on our politics or our moral life in a variety of styles. Men, of course, prefer to argue for the absolute superiority of one code or form. Only in this way can weak human leaders hope to maintain control over the masses. But a God-of-detail is an individualist. He can only deal with us and evaluate and judge us on a one-to-one basis. Immanuel Kant feels more secure with a God who enforces a universal moral law. But, although the stars run in a relatively fixed order, where men and women are concerned, God seems to have elected a more individual approach.

Of course, all this means that we must revise our notions about finding a final proof for God's existence in the natural world. We can argue for God from a general observation of purpose in nature or from cause-effect relationships. Such an argument may lead us to uniform principles, but it will not get us to God. He must be looked for carefully, quietly, observantly in small and subtle places. Thus, the pursuit of God can neither be generalized or universalized or finally concluded. He does not appear in our life in a way that makes this possible. The best overall plan of the universe may not show much of the divine touch, but the intricacy of the design in the subtle detail may.

God's refusal to appear only in mass celebrations, and his preference for care in the detail, explains much about our recurrent religious disappointments. When some subtle note or word or act suddenly stirs us deeply, we often think our insight has come from the situation we are in. Then, we think if we join that group or repeat that external setting this will sustain the momentarily powerful insight.

Alas, God is more easily lost than he is found, and his presence is always hard to sustain. Some subtlety of the moment stirred us, some special sensitivity on our part made us receptive. But above all, God refuses to be bound by any formula. This means that mere repetition ironically kills the possibility of his reappearance.

However, if sensitivity to individual detail is the right approach, we can at least learn how to train our eyes. Mass religious displays or the regular routine of ritual are all right, if one finds profit there. However, God will not be found on the surface of anything. He appears only as our senses become attuned to subtle detail and small facts, and even then with no certainty.

With a good IBM machine any architect could design the general frame of the world. But the world of art and architecture and religion exists because the possibilities for intricacy in detail are endless. God must have taken infinite care with the nuances of creation, even though he could have gotten a world going with much less attention to detail. Evidently the only real link between God and man lies in the subtlety of the detail in our relationship. Thus, we never find God in universal laws or on the surface of the world.

XIV. GOD IS . . .

ABLE TO STAY BEHIND THE GOSPELS

The nineteenth century sparked "The Quest for the Historical Jesus." We thought divinity could be located if we understood the record of history properly. The hopes and the assumptions behind this quest outlined for us the assumptions of that century. But, as the twenty-first century approaches, it is clear that that quest did not recover the "pure Jesus" it hoped for. Perhaps the tools of historical scholarship were not as powerful as we thought, or perhaps we sought the wrong person behind the Gospels.

To find the human, historical Jesus of the gospel stories would actually solve few religious problems for us. We need to know who stands behind him; and God as such hardly appears in the New Testament narratives. Jesus speaks about him in various ways, but, except for a few words from heaven on the occasion of Jesus' baptism, God stays behind the scenes. Jesus remains just another religious figure—unless we can locate the God behind the Gospels.

Our direct evidence is minimal, and even the accounts of Jesus' life are multiple. At the outset we know that we can never find one picture of God that all who listen to the gospel stories will agree upon. Still, it is crucial that the quest be undertaken, and perhaps each age will see God somewhat differently. Or, to put it in another way, perhaps God turns a different face to some generations. If so, we must relocate and redescribe his face. Otherwise, God remains distant and voiceless in our time. We cannot decide who Jesus was or what he did independent from a search for God. Jesus comes alive for us only as we succeed in filling in the picture of the God who stood behind him.

As almost everyone agrees, Jesus' references to God are in explicitly personal terms, e.g., Father, Good Shepherd, etc. Although God does not appear directly, Jesus talks as if he is on familiar terms with him. Jesus finds no difficulty in voicing the message God wants expressed. But the details about the words Jesus uses are unimportant, since Jesus does nothing to establish a definitive, precise, canonical text that contains his doctrine securely.

In fact, Jesus seems to prefer to push the interpretive burden off onto the individual rather than to make every meaning clear for the listener. His use of indirect techniques, storytelling and parables, all indicate Jesus' lack of concern for simple and direct expression. Obviously Jesus' disciples did not understand him, nor did they comprehend God's plan fully at the time. Later, perhaps, they could make clear affirmations about God's intentions, as Paul does. But neither Jesus' presence nor his words about God cleared up the uncertainty at the time.

God must like retrospective understanding and have little concern for making his program clear in advance. The certainty men strive for reflects their own uncertainty, and their desire to overcome it, not God's concern for security. Nothing in the Gospels leads us to a God who fears to take a risk or who determines the future with absoluteness. Furthermore, he seems to be a God capable of deep feeling and of being affected by human actions. Compassion is a key factor in his emotional life, and he does not hesitate to take a difficult path even when loss and bloodshed may be involved. The way is made neither easy nor obvious for his followers. The ethics of his action, as Jesus represents it, allows for individual variation. He must prize variety above conformity in his people.

In the Gospels we do not get a very clear impression of God's closeness to either formal religious institutions or their leaders. Certainly, Jesus worked independently from "the system" of religion in his day. He never left it, but he did not join it professionally either. The God-of-the-Gospels appears critical of ecclesiastical argument but concerned for the people involved in the religious system as well as for those outside its official confines. Thus, any God we restrict to ecclesiastical channels cannot be the God standing behind Jesus, even though he may be seen as such by some churches.

The God behind the Gospels seems full of power, although he uses it very little to intervene. Often he is simply silent. True, the New Testament is full of miracles, but they are a "special show" and not the way God acts every day. The divine response to insult is seldom thunder. The God of the gospel stories does not seem concerned about where he sits at official, state, or church functions. If he is an author of religious doctrine, he is very silent and modest about it all.

Although full of power, the God who could cause the Gospels to be written was capable of accepting death without responding in violence. Such passive behavior disoriented those who expected more from God by way of defiant leadership. His disciples particularly expected more support from God when they agreed to join Jesus' new religious movement. But even when God wants to show his power over death, it is not done so decisively that none can doubt his power. In fact, even today many remain unconvinced that God is really behind the gospel story.

At the very least we have to admit that millions discover his presence elsewhere than in the Gospel accounts. Any God-of-the-Gospels, then, does not give us doubt-proof revelations of himself. He is capable of being missed and misunderstood. Evidently he can operate in a variety of contexts, not just one. Any God behind Jesus must be both quite flexible in his nature and cautious about taking any direct action over the heads of men and women in order to enforce his wishes.

XV. GOD IS . . .

ABLE TO LEAVE US WITH OUR TASK

God appears in many ways. Thus, it is our task to discern the many faces of God—or to find an acceptable picture of God among the many Gods. God does not do this for us. Men have, I suspect, always been aware of the multiplicity of the ways in which they have seen God, but today our task is more difficult and also more challenging. For centuries we pursued the holy grail: the notion that soon, eventually, we would discover God himself among the Gods, or validate the one face among the many as truly God. It was a modern, rationalist hope, but it tends to end in either atheism or vicious self-destruction.

If we search for certainty and finality where none is possible, we turn into fanatic zealots who try to create certainty where it does not exist. We revolt against one God when many Gods are all around us. Determined to find the One with certainty, we overlook the Many. Today our task is no longer the fruitless search for a final elusive unity but the attempt to find God where he lives, in plurality and diversity. This does not, as we shall see, mean that God is everything all men have ever said he is. That suggestion is both repugnant and impossible. Since the suggestion is that his reality lies in his plurality, first, we must accept every face of God suggested to us before we can hope to find what God is like. What we must explain is how God's nature makes it possible for him to be seen in so many ways.

God must be such, then, that he has left it to us to specify his nature. With the vast range his nature covers, he cannot be one thing. Rather, in himself he maintains an infinite richness and flexibility. He can appear and be grasped as one thing at one time, but this does not preclude his being apprehended and described in a slightly different way at another time. One who fails to understand God's tendency to become many Gods is left with an empty shell. God moves on, and we are left wondering why a once vital mode of God's appearance now seems so lifeless. Saying this does not commit us to accept equally every way in which God has been presented, but it does mean that the task is ours to specify God from among the many Gods. God is able to leave that job to us.

He has not specified his nature for us, and that very fact is the central clue to his internal life as he knows himself. How can we, then, accept this and not fight against it? How can we proceed to set up the criteria necessary to select out the acceptable faces of God from among the many Gods, because admittedly, some divinities are hideous and destructive, and against these we must learn to protect ourselves. To begin with, we must elect a focal point, some word or action of God which seems to us to be a central clue which he has given out. Once selected, we can use this as a stabilizing reference point to sort out all that has been and can be said about the multiple faces of God. But given the original diverse core of divinity, no such sorting or stabilizing process can ever be final.

No one is prevented from claiming that he has discovered God in one true face—in one experience, in one setting, or as emerging from one form of practice. Indeed, given the lack of rigid cohesiveness in God's nature, it is necessary for men to claim to have found such a focus. Otherwise one God will never be known personally in distinction from all the many faces. The meaning of faith is to make such an affirmation. We call it faith just because obviously no God is ever the sole possible center of religious attention. No one God stands out from among our experiences of many Gods, including those negative, disappointing, and even destructive experiences. Only if men cling tenaciously to one face as revelatory does God stand still and appear. Relax your grasp and that one face disappears.

Not all God's appearances are due to human effort. He may appear with power at any time and place of his choosing, e.g., with Moses in the burning bush, with Jesus, with the Buddha, or even with Sun Myung Moon. But these divine interventions are misinterpreted and will disappear if we think that God remains either at one place or is alive only within the account of certain events. Because his form is not permanent, he is seldom present very long in any appearance.

One can say God appeared, that he spoke or acted, but one cannot say either that he always remains at that place or that all future divine disclosures must be given exactly in this mode. "God is free" is our major proposition, and thus men are free in their response too. God is only bound to be what he has been, not what he may become. He does not deny his past, as men sometimes do. He remains steadfast to his former word, but he makes no promise to us not to utter new ones.

All appearances of God's face must be considered the result of a joint effort of God and man. Karl Barth is notorious for wanting to free God from man's shackles, leaving God free to be himself. God is free, of course, and he can appear as he wishes, but this freedom does nothing for God if no one recognizes his presence. Recognition is man's business, and without it even the most powerful God seems dead as far as his influence on human life is concerned. Could God force us to recognize his existence? Yes, of course. Any God worth the title could. But his basic characteristic of freedom—one which millions recognize with peculiar forcefulness today—keeps him from pressuring and coercing men, just because he himself rejects such intimidation.

The most powerful divine appearance or act can pass away, without exerting any human influence, if it goes unrecognized and unresponded to. In Jesus' case, most men did not recognize the significance of Jesus' life and words at the time. This is often true with divine appearances, that only in looking back does one begin to grasp the significance of God's appearance.

If the God who appeared always disclosed exactly the same face, the role of human response might be less significant. But since our task is to discern one God from among many Gods, such refining and selecting is man's chief religious function. The pictures presented by the appearances of many Gods are diverse, yet in comparative religious studies we try to synthesize them all.

But God smiles. He knows that if we ever see one God, it will be because we have learned to deal with and are responding to what by nature is plural and never fully specified in itself. Such a situation frustrates our plans to domesticate God by putting all religions together, but it offers a more interesting life for God. Through plurality and diversity he achieves a freedom that a single face would never grant him.

GOD IS NOT . . .

I. GOD IS NOT . . .

ABLE TO BECOME NOTHING

Children learn about their parents, as well as about themselves, by exerting pressure and evaluating the responses given to them. The young need to learn how far they will be allowed to go in their actions and in their speech. Adults reach understanding, too, when they realize the limits beyond which they cannot go, when they understand what it is they cannot do. God would lack self-understanding if he could not recognize what he knows already, that is, what it is that he cannot do. His divine limitations define his nature for us just as much as knowing what he can do. God could not remain himself if he did not work in and through these self-imposed limitations on his power.

There are good reasons why God finds himself restricted. Not to be able to do some things is just as necessary a quality as to be able to exercise certain abilities. Almost as many forms of power are destructive as are constructive, therefore the exercise of some powers is to be avoided. For instance, the opportunity to build human society on the basis of freedom would not be possible if God did not set limits on himself. Without self-restraint, God would overpower us all.

For our sake as well as for his, he denies himself some acts that he could engage in. He could indulge himself, but if he did, he would plunge his own life into chaos and the world into oblivion. Wherever and whenever we resist the devastating forces that lead to destruction, we join God as an ally. In the midst of this resistance movement, we may recognize God as our silent, but powerful, partner. Both of us seek to set restrictions in order to call a halt to chaos-producing subversion.

God, however, cannot reduce himself to nothing. This is not because he could not move to block off his own powers and thus reduce himself to impotence and the world to chaos. God could self-destruct just as men do. But he sets himself against all dissipation of power. He checks any inclination to drift in this direction in the way human beings let themselves go on toward destruction. Given God's powers of calculation, he could design a perfect plan by which he would suppress all his powers at once and so self-destruct.

Instead, God's own natural direction sets him toward positive construction. His every move need not be positive, however. If it were, the world would not be covered with the vast waste that constantly threatens to spoil it. Still, the directional flow of God's nature makes him unable to reduce himself to nothingness in spite of the fact that not all powers in him or in the world are constructive.

We overlook this inability of God to become nothing because sometimes he does disappear from our view. To experience such absence amounts to the same thing as God's becoming nothing. When God evaporates from our lives, particularly if he has once been powerfully present, his absence leaves us with the psychological impression that we are lost in a void. However, God's self-limitation of such radical behavior always leaves open the possibility of his return, even to the places where his absence has been most deeply felt. His disappearance is painful. Of course, his departure causes some to celebrate because they are glad to be rid of him; the modern age even hoped to make his absence permanent. The accompanying pain or joy is always brief, because God never lets himself drift out beyond all recall as we human beings do. He can return when he wants to, and he often does.

Science fiction is a phenomenon of the modern age and is an unpredicted by-product of our scientific advance. We humans have always had a vivid sense of imagination, but the dawn of modern science opened new horizons for us to indulge our speculative bent. Even God is enchanted with the literature science has inspired. He responds to it with more enthusiasm than to the weird notion of his own death.

Given the fantasies and inventiveness of the stories by science-fiction writers, it is not hard to imagine a tendency on God's part to drift toward destruction. We can imagine this, but at the same time God knows he can hold himself in control and continue on in existence. The TV special that dramatizes the problems God has with himself is yet to be made. He retains the power to conquer the forces within that threaten to destroy his life. God finds Hollywood-style movie endings, where the best man always wins, not surprising to him. After all, that is the way he writes his own script.

ABLE TO REJECT ANYTHING

All of us spend part of our lives trying to reject the responsibility that is thrust on us. Adam blames Eve; Cain is sure that Abel is at the root of all his difficulties. Both in public and in private, vast amounts of energy go into trying to prove, either to others or to ourselves, that our own error is someone else's fault. God cannot bring himself to do this. His creative powers force him to accept responsibility for every existing creature, for every thought and action, before his eyes. He could have prevented whatever comes before his gaze. He could have structured it in some other way. God senses his power all too keenly, but for this reason he rejects nothing. He accepts all. His awareness of sin surpasses human understanding.

God is all things. All power in the world, whether it enhances or destroys life, reflects some facet of his nature, because nothing that exists need be as it is had God cared to prevent it. No matter how attractive or deplorable some aspects of life may be when considered in themselves, nothing could be part of our existence if God were not himself in part like that. Yet even what we see and judge at any given moment can never give us a full picture of God's nature. To assess his net worth is more complex and may have to include future intentions that are not yet fully operative. Nevertheless, God rejects nothing as unrepresentative of some part of his nature. If we search his depths long enough, we can locate the source of both the best and the worst in existence.

When we understand that God is not allowed to reject

anything, that everything under the sun finds its origin in his nature, this helps us comprehend both the vastness and the complexity of his being. At the same time, one of the fondest human hopes is taken from us. God, if he rejects nothing, can never appear as one or as pure goodness. His multiplicity is nonreducible.

If only unity, purity, and simplicity lay at the core of his nature, both God and man could rest more easily. If this age-old dream of God's simplicity could be realized, we could resolve so much that is perplexing. Our mind would be able to rest transfixed in simplicity whenever it saw God. Of course, man keeps trying to reduce God to some unity so that he can be known in an easy way. It is just that God eludes all our attempts to tie him down in only one way.

God's inability to reject anything burdens him to accept all things as having their source in his nature. Unfortunately, even if God appears to us, this means no single apprehension of him can ever be final. Our understanding will always continue to shift where God is concerned. This is not due simply to a lack of mental power on our part. It reflects the fact that God's nature is too complex and too full for us ever to rest our hold on him such that he would be incapable of being grasped in any other way.

If we want to apprehend an object simply, we must reject much and fix on some single core. We are pleased with ourselves as human beings when we can do this. In God's case, this is not possible. To simplify, to reject too much, is to miss him, or at least it means we will lose him later even though we have caught him for a minute now. We may grasp some comfortable, substitute divinity, but we have not found the creator God who accepts everything as his own representation.

Mystics seek to identify with a unity that lies beyond the plural surface of the world. The attraction of this goal is due to the blissful rest that union with a principle beyond the world produces. Zen Buddhism goes further. It aims to discipline its followers to break through to a nothingness that lies beyond the division between unity and plurality.

Although hard to attain, it is a blissful, releasing state. One who masters Zen meditation is set free from normal restraints. And God has often considered joining the Zen monks in their seated meditation. He envies both the Zen master and the devotee of John of the Cross. Unfortunately, he is too involved with men and women and the universe to indulge himself in the luxury of such a quiet state.

God can assume the lotus position and spend an eternity in contemplation. He can at will empty his mind of all thought and see the nature of the world as it is without words or any form of meditation. He can learn any meditative technique you care to name better than any man or woman, but he doesn't have much time for such self-centered activity. The demands his creation puts on his nature and the complexity of the projects he has undertaken keep God away from unity and rest.

God cannot escape the task of keeping constant control on complexity. In fact, he rather enjoys it. No matter how diverse or tension-filled it becomes, the world never moves away from his grasp. And he never avoids it or shirks its constant burden. He rejects nothing. He accepts all as originating in him.

III. GOD IS NOT . . .

ABLE TO CONTROL THOSE
WHO REPRESENT HIM

The greatest difficulty we have in discovering what God is like is our tendency to turn first to God's self-proclaimed religious representatives. This seems like a natural place to start, for we expect to meet God in the sacred person or in the church setting more than in the secular world. We tend to believe—or at least to look to—those who tell us they are authorized by God to speak and to represent him to us, particularly if they speak with some credibility. The problem is that religion attracts its share of crazy spokesmen. Yet it is not so much the nonsense of various religious claims that frustrates us, as the fact that even good religions and trustworthy prophets are irreducibly multiple. They do not all speak with a unified voice. Can God be heard in dissonance as well as in silence?

Some who profess to be religious guides are charlatans and fakes from the beginning. Where humanity's concerns are deep and important, con men always lie in wait to build fortunes by pandering to those needs. Even the falseness in much popular religion can provide temporary relief; it just does not last. The history of all religions is full of shocking conduct and human destruction as well as heroic acts and inspiring stories. Like all important endeavors carried on in God's name, in spite of all that is false, there may even be a core of truth and spiritual aid in God's popular religious representatives.

No one can make headway in an important venture if he cannot distinguish the genuine from the sham. And, if we let our anger over what proves false make us mad, we may overlook what is true but lies under the surface. Organized religions have great difficulty in gaining and holding popular acceptance as God's spokesmen. This is not simply because institutional religion is not always pure. In any organization or profession, we must reject many candidates before we locate a representative who can be trusted. Religion is no worse than any other human enterprise. It just is seldom much better, but naively we think it should be.

God cannot control those who represent him, or at least he does not seem to want to. Some spokesmen claim to operate directly under God's authorization. Our problem is that more than one voice announces this, and we never can form a complete unity among all the varied claims. God could control his representatives by ordaining a kind of divinely instituted state church on a worldwide basis. Such a church would need a fixed ecclesiastical hierarchy with direct contact to heaven at the top and each function affixed with a Good Housekeeping seal of approval. Of course, some claim that God favors one man or a particular church, or that his newest personal message resides with some attractive revivalist. Even so, we cannot deny that he allowed the religions of the world to be myriad, multiple, irreducible, and even conflicting.

Impurity in the priestly strain makes it impossible to use his self-proclaimed representatives as our sole model for understanding God. It could be that, personally and privately, he favors one brand more than another. Or, it may be that he is more fully present in some religious events than in others. Still, we must decide for ourselves where to look, and we do not have the advantage of having an authorized agent to determine the right direction for us. He leaves us on our own with the choice of how to find original avenues to God.

If God does not fix an exclusive line of communication with one religion of the world, no single locus is given from which to search for God. Still, each of us is free to testify that he or she finds God in one place more than in another. God may be as secular as he is sacred, although surely he is not irreligious. This need not mean that God can be found equally everywhere. He may elect special places of sensitivity, divine "erotic zones," where care and stimulation at that point produce a more intense response.

Nevertheless, if God does not control his representatives, it is not because he lacks the power to enforce such heavenly censorship. It is just that to do so would be false to his own nature. The presence of a controlled and rigid ecclesiastical monopoly would not reflect God's nature accurately. In fact it would distort his image. If he does not limit himself to one form of life, it would be ultimate hypocrisy for God to establish orthodoxy among his representatives. The existing confusion among religious tongues tells us something about God's original intention for his creatures and what life with such a divine parent must be like.

Given God's penchant for organization, it is strange that he allowed chaos and such a wide range of novelty to characterize the religions that celebrate him. Of course, if he is not totally identified with the life of any one religion, no priest can please him fully nor any sacrifice satisfy all of his demands. We seek God in all our various religions. But perhaps the reason we never find him fully or with finality is because his total life is not lived on the religious dimension alone.

Only part of God is ecclesiastically oriented. Surely he is more religious than not, or else we could accuse him of being false to the various spiritual revelations he has allowed or given. If it is the Godhead we seek and not one particular God, no single form of religious life can satisfy us fully. We must pursue every religious avenue open to us. All the while we know that religious forms and rituals are a human crutch which God does not need in order to approach himself. He may enjoy some ceremonies and sermons, but he resists being fully identified with any one of them.

IV. GOD IS NOT . . .

ABLE TO ELIMINATE ANGER

The God who appears in the Old Testament stories either cannot, or at least does not care to, control his anger. We have many accounts of God's activity which evidence his ability to become angry. These are sometimes labeled as primitive pictures and are said to be no longer valid for modern man. Newer and more sophisticated views of God's nature assume that to eliminate all anger is a sign of progress. They portray God as serene, loving, calm, and wrapped in blissful silence. In a real sense, he is above all the world's strong passions, and such a quiet God-of-contemplation has an attraction for us all, especially when the world's bedlam becomes too much. However, is God actually able to eliminate his anger and live the easy life we like to imagine for him?

One good reason why we want to place God above passion is that so much human anger is petty and selfish. We get mad when our egos are offended or when our pride is hurt. When human anger stems from insecurity and a concern for our self-interest, our anger is unworthy of God. We come up against enough tough, petty individuals on earth without finding one in heaven too. Thus, what we might say is that God neither gets angry over an affront to his dignity nor reacts to a challenge to his rights and privileges. He possesses a personal security we do not have. The divine reaction to any threat from us is likely to be laughter rather than anger.

On what occasions, then, might God not be able to control his anger? To discover what these sensitive spots are is as revealing about him as it is about us. If God never gets angry when he is attacked, perhaps it is only any unfairness or brutality toward other human beings which causes an unrestrained fury to rise up in him. If God never uses another person solely for his own advantage, any violation of human dignity and integrity will infuriate him. If his anger rises whenever men become selfishly vicious, a great deal in the human scene will make God mad and disrupt the tranquility of heaven. We discover much about divinity when we learn what human acts he considers beyond the pale of toleration.

We men and women hide a great deal behind a discreet smile and a locked door, but God does not blush easily. Sex surely cannot offend him, since he is the author of that complex game. He is responsible for the depths as well as the heights to which that passion so easily leads us. Sex must mean a lot to God, too, or else he would have muted its prominence in our thought and action and not let it occupy so much human emotion and energy. Even when sex leads us into sordid situations, this in itself does not make God angry.

As in all things, divine anger rises only when a natural desire is so misused that others are destroyed or made into slaves for the satisfaction of our pleasure. If we are ruthless in our disregard for the injury we cause others in the pursuit of our own self-interest, in that situation God finds sex pornographic. Only then is he unable to eliminate his anger over the interpersonal abuse involved. This is true whether the humiliation involved is in sex or economics or politics or religion. Blind desire blindly satisfied begets divine anger.

Speculation about "the day God lost control of anger" would make a marvelous doomsday plot. However, it is a little beyond the mind's power to visualize the result of God's total loss of self-restraint. Anger has its satisfying as well as its humorous aspects, and there is no more reason to deny anger to God than laughter. In fact, the two should go together. When he is provoked, God toys with the vision of letting his anger go just as we do. Nevertheless, entertaining as it is to contemplate such a scene, God is unable to let himself get out of control. He settles for a momentary evidence of his anger as well as this can be reflected in the world.

What we now humorously call "the primitive mind" understood that God's anger was embodied and expressed all around us. A violent storm probably is not the direct expression of God's voice which early tribes imagined it to be, but it is a better symbol of divine wrath than our more sophisticated religious piety knows how to portray. Only men indulge themselves in explosions as a rash expression of their emotion. Humorous as it may be to consider how God might explode, he laughs at such a thought as he paints it in his imagination. He chooses to express his anger in more subtle forms than in uncontrolled explosion. He is an artist of controlled rage. We tend to be sloppy.

V. GOD IS NOT . . .

ABLE TO LOSE HIMSELF

We human beings fall into sheer panic at the thought of losing ourselves. This is because we know it is easy to become personally disoriented. Even when we are not aware of any explicit danger, our panic level rises over a real or imagined threat to our stability. This is due to a preconscious realization that, if once we become lost, we may not be able to find our way back home.

There are points of no return for the human psyche beyond which it loses all control. If we cross these, we sometimes never quite regain the self we once were. This fear takes many forms, from the crying child lost in the crowd, to the student afraid that if he leaves one professional goal or girlfriend he may never find another, to the pathetic mental patient who gradually cuts himself off from the world but later consciously prefers to remain lost to himself because his fear is so great.

God on the other hand misses the excitement of such risky human ventures. He is forced to enjoy these thrills vicariously. If God had not pushed humanity into a precarious adventure, the amusement world would not be such an exciting and profitable business. Certainly many seek to experience thrill and danger even at the risk of no return. Such daredevils make God's life and ours exciting if often also tragic.

Yet, no matter how far out God may venture, he is not able to lose himself. For us mortals, self-forgetfulness is at times refreshing. The chance to wander alone and unknown is a relief. God knows no such joys; he is ever-present to himself. He cannot escape or cut himself off. Of course he does not know the need we feel to lose some part of ourselves. We cut off our memory in the fear of being destroyed by events too strong for us to handle. God remains always in control. He is unflappable even in the face of atomic explosions, whether internal or external.

If we discover God's inability to lose himself, we realize that a person who wants to lose him or herself, or a person who is already lost, needs God. What such a person lacks is the strength to remain always present to his past at the same time that he is open to his future. If we could maintain self-presence easily, escape to alcoholism, drug addiction, and sexual experimentation would be less widespread. Games and diversions and seductive people help us to forget.

We often want to lose contact with parts of ourselves, with our past, and even with what may lie ahead. Unfortunately, our attempts at selective forgetting often are not very skillful. We lose too much of ourselves in trying to lose that part of us we want to let go of. We sometimes lose our consciousness altogether, when all we wanted was to get rid of an upsetting memory or to avoid the unsettling future that looms ahead.

The power to remain ourselves, to accept all that we have been and may be, and still not to flee in panic—this requires divine strength. Wherever we experience such a power, we are near to God. He is the most accepting being we can ever know, both of himself and of others. This is not because he likes everything about himself or other people. We know that he can get angry over abuse. It is just that he is unable to lose himself in a vain attempt to avoid responsibility, as men and women often do. God can accept all and yet remain himself.

On the other hand, we are sometimes altered beyond belief when we attempt to take in too much. God's reserve capacities are such that he feels no need to lose himself. Our human tolerance level is more precarious and is subject to sudden shifts. To hide nothing from oneself, to accept what we would prefer to hide rather than to try to lose ourselves—to achieve such a state of openness is to reach the level of the divine and to know something about how God lives.

The life of modern man has been absorbed in the search for his self-identity. The theme of alienation and lostness haunts modern poetry and fiction. God reads a lot, and so he knows how we wandering humans feel and how we express this feeling, even if God cannot experience lostness in himself. He has read the novels of Richard Wright and Thomas Wolfe and William Faulkner. In fact, modern man's preoccupation with lostness and the search that results is one reason the modern world has not been able to attune itself to God easily.

We know God cannot drift into a lost state. Thus, if our own search to find self-identity and overcome alienation is successful, it becomes the modern equivalent of knowing God. In the moment we overcome alienation and realize our identity, we understand how God feels. He experiences self-loss only by visiting our theaters, our psychiatrists, our mental hospitals, or by listening to our desperate prayers. His own self-experience is one of constant presence and self-knowledge, but this contrast between the human and the divine is a source of unease to a God who seeks human relationships.

VI. GOD IS NOT . . .

ABLE TO EXCLUDE DESIRE

The attraction of desire is present on every street corner and lurks behind every door. It is a little strange that so many theologians have seen fit to eliminate desire from their descriptions of God. God need not reflect in a major way something that plays a minor role in human life. But what drives men and women either to madness or to ecstasy surely must represent an important part of God's life too. Some think that to admit God knows desire makes him out to be deficient. Any need man has requires something outside himself for its satisfaction, and the traditional goal of theologians has been to maintain God's self-sufficiency.

We thought we should allow him to depend not on others for his fulfillment but only on himself. It is argued that we must attribute a divine, that is, a perfect independence to God in order to secure his control of creation. There is a compelling logic in the traditional demand to "keep God clean" of our faults. Human desires so often go out of control. We too easily become dependent on others—persons, things, or drugs—to satisfy our needs. We even debase ourselves in self-defeating ways while attempting to quench these thirsts. God, then, should not be forced to depend on others, as we so often do to our own disgrace.

However, if God should openly choose to accept dependence and to know desire in his internal life, such a decision would bring him closer to us and tell a tale of amazing divine adventure. In that case God would feel desire because he allowed himself to be put in need of other people for his own fulfillment. In such a relationship, there would be no desire from which he would be totally free. However, such a sense of God's presence is captured in some experiences of dependency more than in others. For instance, love that is offered to another is closer to the life of God than the drug experience, although both involve dependence.

The age-old question of whether Jesus is "fully human as well as fully divine" reduces itself to this issue: Did Jesus know desire? From the New Testament story of his temptation on the mountaintop, we know that Jesus reports feeling the same pulls we do when what is forbidden is offered to him. One cannot claim to be tempted by what arouses no desire or holds no attraction. We need not go so far as some do and imagine a sex life for Jesus. There is nothing sacrilegious in such a thought, since we know God himself was deeply involved in constructing the mechanisms of sex.

However, we fail to understand God if we cannot fathom how Jesus handles his own desires. He felt them, just as God does; that much is sure. Jesus probably felt the power of desire more deeply than some of us do; this is his humanity. But he was not overpowered by those pulls; that is his divinity. This does not mean that Jesus never moved to satisfy his desires. We know he did, because he ate and drank with publicans and sinners. Nevertheless, any desire that is divine in origin never allows itself to be fulfilled selfishly.

On rare occasions, we human individuals conform to this gracious rule, but such self-effacing action is an exception. We become skillful in claiming that our desired satisfactions are also in the best interests of those we need for our fulfillment. We tend to argue that what is good for our satisfaction is also good for others. Sometimes this is happily true. Enjoyment can be mutual, but such coincidence is more rare than our desire-blindness usually allows us to admit.

To know desire, which requires that we take what others have for its fulfillment, to possess the power to coerce, and yet never to fulfill desire selfishly or damage another for our own ends—such control of desire reflects the presence of divine power. If Jesus exercised this constantly in his relationships with others, he was divine. Where we find desire unselfconsciously and unselfishly controlled, we see God. Where we find raw desire powerfully felt and openly responded to, we are with humanity.

Imagine a passionless world. In many ways, to live in such an atmosphere would be a relief, particularly if you have just been driven to distraction by some desire that wouldn't quit. God is sometimes imagined to embody a state that lies beyond the reach of desire. If he is like that, he leaves much of the world unaccounted for. If he really is passionless, then sensational magazines and novels take on proportions which God cannot explain. If God is affected by no internal passion, why does it loom so large in a world he created? Of course, some see the rage of passion as solely the work of the Devil. He is the monster who walks down 42nd Street in New York while God sits quietly at prayer or meditation in St. Patrick's Cathedral.

Yet the very existence of the Devil and his strong passions tells us something about God. Surely the Devil feels no attraction which God does not experience. But he is the Devil just because he cannot control himself and is driven to extreme action in a desperate attempt to gain his needed satisfactions. We may sometimes think of God, then, as an "in control Devil." Nothing any Satan conspires for or urges on us is foreign to God.

God feels all that presses in on us and more. He just does not yield or allow himself to let go. Of course, this means that he does miss the pleasure that comes with an act of absolute abandonment, except as he may experience it vicariously. However, we can be sure that God rejected a passionless world in the beginning as being too unexciting to create. He opted for greater tension and greater excitement but also for greater destruction. He can stand it. Often it seems too much for us.

84

VII. GOD IS NOT . . .

ABLE TO AVOID EVIL

The Gods whose pictures we carry about with us we depict as "pure beings." If we are right, heaven should be both peaceful and easily governed. Strange, isn't it, how we censor God's portrait for our own creature-comfort when we should consider, not what we can stand, but only what God is able to bear. And there is little evidence in history that God either can or wants to avoid all evil. After all, according to the biblical story, the rebellion against God broke out in heaven within the ranks of his own choir. The devil was (is) an angel, as all who have ever been attracted by one know!

If God himself is fully pure, if he does not now and never has known evil, it would make sense to think that the world he created might be like him in kind, even if to a lesser degree. But we know that life in our world is not made up of various shades of goodness. Powerful and destructive forces stalk our every step by night and by day. Heaven must have its problems of law and order too.

Religious leaders and theologians have tried to prove that what we call evil is only a lesser form of good. In spite of this claim, the world we face exhibits powerfully destructive features. If "the godfather" has kindly qualities and a respect for his ancestral religion, the blood bath that spills out around him belies his innocence. "God the Father" may be more agreeable in his motives than the underworldly "godfather," but the Mafia is God's creation too.

If in fact God has strong male, as well as female, characteristics, we cannot go beyond this aspect of God's creation either. Thus, when our world is rocked by a war between male and female forces which are identical neither in kind nor in intent, God experiences these same divisions in his own being. He is able to prevent evil from destroying his nature, but he cannot avoid evil in what he creates. If he could, he would spread a false image of what life with God the Father is really like. Such life is not so much beyond all evil as it is in control of what otherwise would destroy.

If we are forced to admit that the origin of the destructive forces which terrorize us lie internal to God's own nature, we may have to rethink our relationship to God radically. The experiences in which we meet him cannot be the sweet, contemplative, pastoral homecoming we desire when we are exhausted from combat. In the first place, if evil lies at the base of things, spouting both blind and shrewdly calculated destruction, we should face it just as God does and stop trying to explain it away in his name.

We have to learn to treat evil as an internal tendency and power, one that requires constant vigilance and counter-pressure. If we realize that God is not able to avoid evil because the origin of such power is interior to his nature, this teaches us something important about the possible success of any human moral crusade. The enemy may appear to us from outside, but the source of part of his power for any campaign he wages lies internal to our nature and to God's.

Evil, then, could not wield the destructive power against us which it does if we were not split internally. We are so often our own worst enemy as well as our own best ally. If God cannot hold back every expression of evil and still remain honest with himself, at least he never allows himself to become his own worst enemy, as we so often do. He knows friend from foe, while we evidence our human frailty by blindly feeding the flames of our own destruction; we reject friends who only want to help us.

We will miss seeing God if we pretend evil does not have power of its own, or if we try to avoid evil in a way which even God does not do. Actually, we come face to face with

God when we acknowledge destruction's origin as internal to the divine life. Yet, we can never counter evil in such a way that it is finally overcome. All we can do is immunize its destructive powers temporarily. If God cannot avoid evil, how can we hope to?

In your mind's eye, picture heaven as without evil and destruction. This is how many do imagine it. However, the dullness of this vision puts others off. Who wants to go on and on and on with no variation in temperature or emotional pressure? Yet, all of us want to one day escape the constant threat of destruction, and the Christian symbol of the resurrection tells us that we can. But if the origin of evil is interior and if even God cannot escape it, we can never be rid of evil unless we get rid of God too.

In creation, God had to allow some degree of destruction to enter in order to be honest with us, but nothing forced God to allow any certain degree of corrosive evil. Internally, in his own life, he can hold evil expressionless. The symbol of "being in God's own hands" means to be held above destruction. Our new image of heaven, then, should be one of a place of variety. It is a state where everything conceivable can be thought and felt, but the control of all expression still remains in our hands. We can never get rid of the origin of evil, but we can do away with the kind of uncontrolled indulgence that induces destruction. God willing, it can be kept in bounds. That's what heaven is all about.

VIII. GOD IS NOT . . .

ABLE TO PREDICT THE FUTURE

Our own uncertainty about the future leads us to attribute to God a certainty we do not have: a knowledge of future events in their every detail. Uncertainty appears to us as a disadvantage, so we remove it from God by guaranteeing him security in his knowledge of future events. All this represents a gigantic projection onto God of man's own wish-fulfillment. If God is able to handle uncertainty and resist the temptation to enforce his own rigid necessity on events, such an openness to the future might be his greatest joy. Perhaps the openness of the future and the contingencies of freedom are to him worth all the uncertainty they involve.

If so, a world predetermined down to its smallest detail would neither please God nor give him the feeling of power and control we think it should. Predestination might actually frustrate him, because it does not express the core of his own freedom. If God prizes freedom and the contingency of decision and self-control above all else, a world which did not reflect this could not be his creation. A world of eternal fixity would elude his own preferred mode of understanding and cause him pain, just because such a world is so little like him.

If one enjoys freedom and the exercise of contingent decision, nothing is more frustrating than unchangeability. Likewise, nothing could be more exciting than the risk of uncertainty. If we view our future as held open to us, our creative imagination provides a basis for understanding God's enthusiasm over the uncertainties of life. In a precarious world, God sees man acting in his own image. The imago dei is uncertainty, not certainty.

Only the weak, not the strong, avoid uncertainty. Nothing in the future can fall outside God's calculation of the odds for how events might turn out. Contingency presents no challenge to his power, or at least the threat is not enough to force him to slap rigid controls on human behavior. God does not feel the need, as we weaklings might, to eliminate contingent decision or human caprice—even if it is malevolent. To be sure, human behavior is all too disappointingly predictable. Authentic rebels are an exception to the rule.

Prometheus is an oddity among the league of flattering conformers who hover around the divine court—and God is a secret admirer of Prometheus' daring. God keeps open the possibility for an unusual nonconformer and hopes men won't fail him. "God loveth a cheerful rebel." Freedom can be destructive, but the rare and spectacular use of this divine power to open new worlds made God willing to forego plotting out and enforcing a single predictable future. That was too dull and unsportsmanlike an act for a strong being to stoop to.

Of course, some persons acquire a skill in predicting and determining the future. When we are alert, very little surprises us, even if the outcome of events is different from our prediction. So too, God is not shocked by deviations from his own calculations. Neither our capricious behavior nor the uncertainty of the future falls outside the bounds of what he expects. Our idiosyncratic additions amuse him as they unfold. There is in fact all too much predictability in human affairs.

God may be mocked but he cannot be shocked. He knows the limits of possibility, and he is skilled in probability prediction. In fact, he invented the game. Since his self-confidence is high, he can afford to take risks. He feels no need to force us into a system of strict control just to secure his own protection. Actually, we are the ones who plead for a fixed future, not God. His power is fully adequate to sustain himself against uncertainty. To confront the fact that certainty is a human, not a divine, demand is to discover one central feature of God's nature.

Imagine what would happen if God ventured to predict a date for the end of the world, and then found himself wrong. Could he live down the disgrace? I think he would probably laugh about it. He would explain to us that factors once looked to him as if they were headed for a destructive climax. But then all this did not go ahead to happen of its own accord, and he did not want to intervene to bring his expectations about, although he could have. Other factors also entered in which held back the final end. Imagine God with a computer of infinite size and capacity. It answers his questions instantaneously on the basis of the evidence his intelligence gives it.

The problem in predicting the future is that men keep changing the relevant evidence. We could predict the future if we could force one option against all others as God can, but he seldom chooses to live his life that way. The openness of our future reflects God's self-chosen lifestyle. However, we humans make a mistake if we copy this openness but forget that we seldom have sufficient power to control every eventuality, something which God does easily. The future is more fun if we accept it as contingent decisions move it along. Surely life is less a matter of anguish if we accept both its openness and our own limitations of control.

IX. GOD IS NOT . . .

ABLE TO ABANDON THOUGHT

Dionysius, Meister Eckhart, and countless others with a mystical inclination have said that, ultimately, God lives his life above thought. If so, that is, if we must reach him by perfecting some method of contemplation, we must learn to surpass thought. Or, at least we must set thought aside at some point in our divine quest. Of course, we may ask: Does rational, discursive thought really represent an inferior level? If it does, to know God we must move "beyond thought" and its way of dividing and limiting.

However, the way of the mystic assumes that "unity" is God's primary characteristic. It also assumes that all human thought is locked in an impasse which our way of thinking cannot itself resolve. That is a Zen Buddhist claim. But this may or may not be the case. If it is not, to learn that God is unable to abandon all thought is to discover one central fact about his nature. That is, God is inescapably complex in his life and action.

If God is condemned continually to think without letup, this is because the not-yet-determined qualities of his nature require it. That is, a God already set in his ways, one who has the future firmly in his grasp, such a God has no need to think continually. However, if indeterminacy remains and contingency is characteristic of all that is real, to abandon thought would be to risk losing command of the situation. The world of nature is not out of God's control, but it remains in his grasp only because his will refuses to abandon thought. Instead of letting go, his thought works to keep him appraised of all free acts. He has allowed neither his own nature nor man's future to become fixed. This testifies to God's willingness continually to rely on thought as his chosen instrument of adjustment and control.

The indeterminacy of both God's nature and humanity's future requires God to hold on to thought. Our minds, then, are not such inadequate instruments for approaching God as some have said. Of course, if God is unable to abandon thought, this is partly because he cannot rid his life of affection and the results of emotional attachment. Feelings are less subject to rigid control than either physical nature or human thought.

If thought is necessary for God, this tells us something about his existence as a feeling, willing, deciding being. Active thought is a truer expression than the supposed image of the divine life as one of pure contemplation beyond all knowing. God needs thought, as we all do, precisely because his life is made up of more than thought. Only Descartes is essentially a thinking being, not God. Emotion is not an improper avenue of approach to God, although that path is not crowded with philosophers.

Thought can apprehend things of a nature other than or different from its own. Thought of such flexibility testifies to God's complex life and to the infinite aspects which inform it. His attributes or characteristics may not be absolutely infinite, as Spinoza thought they were, but certainly his nature does not hold him neatly to a rigid pattern of uniform action. God needs thought if he is to encompass his own multiplicity and direct his action with an assured measure of control.

Freedom is useless to us unless it is backed up by the calculations which constant thought provides. Those who want necessity to control their lives begin by putting thought aside and depreciating it as representing an inferior level of attainment. On the contrary, God cannot afford not to think. To realize why this is so is to understand something of the dynamics of his nature. God is God because he is alert to follow every new suggestion which thought offers and feelings prompt.

able to abandon thought

It is said that "Zen detests every kind of intellectuality." The lesson we are given in the classical Zen text, *The Ox and the Herdsman*, is this: However far conceptual understanding takes you, it can never grasp the nature of things. This is an interesting viewpoint, and Zen Buddhism is quite powerful in its critique of our uncritical confidence in the power of thought. Zen suggests that thought itself may be our problem. However, even this position must not be adopted uncritically.

The issue is: What is reality like? Ultimately, can it be grasped by thought or not? And what is God like? What role, if any, does thought play in his life? The interesting thing to note is that how we answer these questions does not so much depend on the nature of thought as on the element of freedom and contingency we find in life and also on the importance we assign to emotion and feeling. If God is not determined but is basically free and contingent, he needs thought as an instrument of decision. If reality is partly constructed by free human action, we cannot afford to abandon thought. We sometimes wish we could restrict its role, turn it off or rise above it. But even when thought frustrates us by leading nowhere, our need is to purify it rather than eliminate it.

X. GOD IS NOT . . .

ABLE TO DENY HIS WILL

Theologians often want to eliminate volition from the divine nature because it is such a difficult concept to handle. But think of how God must feel about all this. It would simplify his life greatly, as well as add immeasurably to his pleasure, if he could set his will aside and merely enjoy a secure life of contemplation. Yet, for men and women as well as for God, it is strength of will that provides the crucial ingredient to keep us alert and on course. Will is that element without which human life would fall into fruitless routine. Will is that without which all our good intentions would collapse into the effortless but also unfruitful dreams of youth.

God is eternally young, but not in the sense that he can easily dream up any fulfillment he desires—that favorite pastime of students when the professor's lecture ceases to attract them. God may feel a desire to "get away from it all," but his maturity involves the cold knowledge that, if his will should relax for a moment, the best of his intentions would simply evaporate into a memory.

Will is our key if we want to mold the future to become what we intend for ourselves. God knows this with a clarity we human beings cannot maintain consistently. We need to relax and forget from time to time. But while we relax, like Sampson, we often have our determination subverted. God knows how to use the lightness of humor; he can allow himself to rest from his labors. But his alertness never lapses, nor can his power ever unintentionally be diverted.

While he slept, Sampson's hair was cut, and thus his

strength depleted. We can say that God may smile or grimace, laugh or rest, but he never sleeps. Men and animals alone enjoy this pleasure; God abstains voluntarily. The power which his will releases holds both himself and creation together. If he were ever to deny his will, the world would come down in shambles around his head like Sampson's temple.

We human beings must also depend on other people to maintain their good intentions in the way they promise to do. We stand by and watch the various enterprises of our friends falter, along with our own, whenever we cannot sustain human determination. When we no longer have a desire to go on, or when we shift and think some new course is more advantageous, we are in a dangerous hour. God *could* have a faulty will, such as some men are cursed with, but the stability of nature and the exactitude possible in science argue against this being the case. He is steadfast.

Of course, for God to change his will is not the same as to deny what he has willed before. Occasional shifts are needed, if he is to accommodate to the freely elected decisions men and women make. On the other hand, some of us are stubborn and refuse to change our earlier conclusions even when circumstances have been altered. But such inflexibility gets human beings into just as much trouble as a weak will that can't remain consistent.

God has the flexibility he needs to adjust to novelty. He maintains an agility most men lose with age, although he never denies his will once it is committed. It will never be necessary to sue God for breach of contract or charge him with failure to deliver on a promise. Nevertheless, the results of what he wills are neither fully visible now nor entirely finished in their form. God's actions always tend toward some future climax, one which he counts on his will to sustain when the time arrives.

The successors of Christ who claim the title of the head of his visible church are also the successors to the man who denied Christ three times during his trial. This symbol reminds us of the fact that, no matter how adamantly men protest their loyalty, the human scene is as much built on betrayal and denial as it is on steadfastness. Jesus sensed this irresoluteness in his devoted followers. Yet, he neither ranted or raved against it nor tried to prevent it.

Any church and its leadership is built of frail substance, but a religious community can serve a divine purpose in spite of its fallibility. Evidently God is able to accept an imperfect religious situation and still work with the changes and infirmities inherent in the human will. God will never deny his own will once it is committed, but he has elected to work through creatures who differ with him most noticeably in their lack of this quality. To change one's mind is human; to remain steadfast in decision is divine.

XI. GOD IS NOT . . .

ABLE TO ACCEPT COERCION

God's attitude toward the use of brute force may at first seem a little strange. Anyone who possesses the unlimited power he does certainly is at liberty to achieve his ends in any way he wills. Only we whose reserves are questionable and precarious become calculating and shy about employing power. We frail humans must be cautious to be sure we do not stir up a reaction that goes beyond our ability to contain it. Since God can handle any rebellion he chooses to confront, he is free to use his power as he wills. Why, then, does he refuse to use coercion to accomplish his ends? Men and women observe no such scruple, and God is a being, not of placidity, but of potentially devastating power.

In order to understand this self-restraint on God's part concerning the use of force, we must look, not to power alone, but to God's other attributes. God embodies the basic qualities of a person, that is, understanding, will, power, emotion. Thus, he is a respecter of persons. It would violate the limits he has established for himself if he allowed power to dominate his nature. To use force on someone outside himself might accomplish his intent in an overt way. Still, to do so would destroy the integrity of the person against whom such superior force might be deployed. God could simply order each individual in the world of nature to obey. If he did, destruction which is now so rampant could be curtailed, but in the process all initiative and freedom would also be blocked. He could do this, although he seldom uses such power even when it is available. We humans are less scrupulous in our attempts to coerce.

Of course, it is clear that God does not prohibit the use of all force. The destructive powers that run wild in the world give lavish testimony to his steel-like nerve. He turns lesser destructive powers loose on us, but these are only the minor powers in his arsenal. Still, they are sufficiently destructive to annihilate millions. Why, then, does he hesitate to use his personal force on us, especially when his aims are so much more admirable than ours and thus deserve every advantage available?

The challengers would not be evenly matched in such a game of strength. God, who has the power needed to save us, ironically is handicapped in his effectiveness, because he eschews all force that involves the destruction of human integrity. His good intentions to help us are weakened by virtue of a divine decision to forego the use of coercion. He seems a strange God who places himself and us in such an unnecessarily vulnerable position.

How can we explain this oddity? We have said that God does not allow himself to use force against persons to insure their compliance. He sometimes moves against destruction, but for the present he does so only with one hand tied behind his back. Nothing ultimately prevents him from acting to reduce to helplessness all the brutality in humanity and in nature. He can force us to come within his control, because he remains free and in command of his will. For now, however, God attempts to reach his goals without the use of force, because he is a respecter of persons. Yet this restraint places an incredible burden on our human ability to respond to the excessive demands placed on us with any emotion other than hate. God leaves us free to face a sometimes devastating choice.

The novels we read, the newspaper accounts of crime and politics are full of stories about the force one person imposes on another. Even when applied for constructive vs. destructive purposes, pressure is the name of the game for those who want to get ahead. If no one used force against another, what would fill our TV screens each day?

How can what is a fact of our life be shunned by God in his own activity? We know that he could win the game of power-play without even trying.

We often accomplish good things by applying pressures, and sometimes this works. But as often as not we destroy or cripple someone by our use of excessive force. God accepts the risk of using a less direct avenue to his goal because he will not damage another person even for his own laudable purposes. He does this even though his self-restraint often means loss by default. God would make a poor novelist or politician. He shuns what we consider an essential part of the human way of life. Occasionally God acts in a way dramatic enough for newspaper copy, but on the whole he plays a quiet waiting game. In fact, God is so unobtrusive that many overlook both his presence and the potential power he holds in trust for the future.

XII. GOD IS NOT . . .

ABLE TO BE CAPTURED IN ONE WAY

Divinity is by nature elusive. We pursue human self-understanding with intensity, and our attempts to know other people are equally fascinating. Little do we realize that God is the most difficult of all beings to pin down. This is not due to sheer perversity on his part. He has no fear as we do about being committed. He may shift and move away, just as our net of understanding is about to come down around him, but this is not an elaborate sport on his part which he plays simply to indulge in the art of gamesmanship. We have a horror of being tied down if we give out a too open disclosure of our thought and activity. Our freedom might be compromised by such outside scrutiny. The reasons for God's elusiveness are different.

His nature does not, as has sometimes been said, exceed our grasp because it lies beyond human conception. Men can think any thought about God they want to. We are, however, more like him in mind and in affection than in body. Yet, we must begin with the body—an aspect we miss which tends to throw us off balance at the start of our search. Although we may at first try to hold on to him with a single concept, whether it be Good or Unity or Holiness, God is too complex to be grasped that easily. If we could unite a constellation of concepts and attributes in our mind at one time, this would come the closest to letting us hold on to God.

The irony is that such a multiplicity of concepts has no inherent fixity beyond a moment. A loose collection may hold momentarily but then will shift and become inadequate as an instrument to grasp God, particularly if we do not constantly adjust our ideas. We need to hold our thoughts in exactly the right balance for each new situation. If God does not always choose to hold the same relationship to the world, we will need to change our fixed concepts from time to time. This required subtlety is easily overlooked if we are not careful. Oddly enough, we tend to treat God too simply to do justice to his vast and complex nature. This is true even though he does hold himself in a unity of thought and action.

In spite of the fact that God does not live beyond all thought, the concepts we use do not carry enough energy to hold him still while our thought grasps him. Concepts have flexibility and a capacity to create both pleasure and powerful human insight, but we often confuse the power of a concept with the insight and pleasure it arouses. When we do this, we are misled if we expect to capture God using the same tools others have used. That is, we cannot simply repeat again a once successful formula.

It is disconcerting for us to learn that what worked to lead some to God may not work for us in the same way in our time. Then, in sullen reaction, we assert either that the formula is not valid or that the ritual is false and cannot evoke God. Actually, what happened is that we mistook the discovery of what was a once-effective avenue for a few as a guarantee that all could accomplish an intricate journey successfully. We forgot that God does not always respond to the same call or submit to the same intellectual approach each time. He would be false to his nature if he did.

This lack of consistency is not because God is moody and perverse. On the contrary, if he allowed his nature to be held in strict identification with any one verbal expression or ritual act, this would be easier for us. But we would also be misled. This is particularly true if we expect God to appear automatically when certain words are uttered or specific acts are done. If he did this, it might give us the idea that our concepts hold more power than they do.

However, we all know that the right words can do wonders on the right occasions—even for God.

Nevertheless, he cannot allow himself to be captured in any one way or domesticated by any liturgical routine. To do so would deprive him of his most prized attribute, freedom. This freedom which he guards—not to appear if he so chooses—is as disconcerting to our desire for security as it is essential to the exercise of his power. On the other hand, it also makes him free to overlook the score in the human game—if he wants to. Because he keeps himself beyond our verbal control, he remains free to release the power needed to save us all—if he will.

For centuries now, each new religion and each new spiritual leader has offered us a formula for capturing God. Each one tells us: All you need to do is follow the way I have outlined. Amazingly enough, many of these suggestions do work. When they do, a new religious movement is born. The perplexing thing about the formulas outlined for pinning God down is that there is more than one, and their number continues to increase. Furthermore, even classically successful ways to approach God grow cold with time. Religious fervor once held at a fever pitch will cool with age. Even vivid religious insights fade.

God clearly intended no one spiritual path to remain open all the time. If we accept this conclusion, we know we should never rely too rigidly on any past success, whether it is one we have developed ourselves or that of some religious seer. We are continually forced to search out for ourselves new avenues to God that fit the time, the place, and the people. God relates himself to time in various ways; therefore this does not mean that all approaches we map out will be equally valid or successful, nor does it mean that everyone who claims to offer us a way to God has actually found him. All it means is that the search for God requires a constant state of alertness and a keen sense for the novel.

XIII. GOD IS NOT . . .

ABLE TO DENY THE HOLOCAUST

It is not intellectual speculation but devastating destruction that has recently raised the question of God for us. Descartes' arguments intrigue some who have a philosophical turn of mind and who are disposed to consider proofs for God's existence. Saint Anselm's "ontological argument" still remains a constant source of intellectual controversy. For the public at large, however, it is the recent tales of horror and mass destruction that have raised questions about God most vividly. This is particularly true for Jews who suffered the most dramatic and publicized holocaust at the hands of the Nazis.

Still, we all know that holocausts have gone on in other lands involving other peoples not quite so marked by religion. Thus, all ideas of cultural progress, or the gradual uplift of humanity along a scale of increased sophistication, must be abandoned. We know horror comes from the intellectually advanced as well as from the primitive. Destruction knows no time or place. It is as much at home in universities as in primitive villages.

Where God and human loss are concerned, it is interesting to note that passing through wanton destruction does not automatically remove all belief in God. However, it does not make belief automatic either. The letters and records of those who move through these experiences show some who disintegrate and lose all semblance of belief and some whose belief in God is radically transformed but deepened.

As we might suspect, nothing remains quite the same after a whirlwind of destruction has passed by. But the torrent of writing, TV spectaculars, etc. now available on the holocaust indicates that such a devastating experience can be productive. It is hard to imagine Solzhenitsyn without the *Gulag Archipelago*. Would Elie Wiesel have become a storyteller if he had been left to grow up quietly in a remote East European village and not been uprooted by the winds of destruction?

Still, the productivity of such an experience—when it does not destroy those involved totally—is not my particular point. What kind of God is compatible with such an experience of waste and destruction and the degradation of human life? Certainly if you live beyond an experience of total death one result is a new view of life and God. Most obviously, all easy and sweet views of God disappear, as do all notions that somehow religious belief will protect the believer and automatically grant him his heart's desire.

In any holocaust the good suffer with the bad, the pious along with the disbeliever. And the function of prayer must be rethought too. Thousands, if not millions, have prayed to God for delivery from threatened destruction. Only a few survive, and surely this includes some who did not even implore God to release them. Furthermore, the direct involvement of God in human affairs can't be very extensive, and at best it is infrequent. Nor can his infrequent appearances be very closely correlated to times of desperate need. He may make himself available to individuals at isolated times, but his direct intervention certainly is minimal.

However, it is the status of evil in God's nature which forces on us a reconception of divinity. Certainly one may cease to believe in God as a result of experiencing the overwhelming evil of a holocaust. When this happens, a failure to explain the presence of evil satisfactorily may be the cause. For evil now lies close to God, in that minor evils can be explained with distance from God and can be attributed to God's intention to provide us with moral instruction, but major, wanton destruction serves no recognizable purpose. And if it is so pervasive, it must lie close to God's central design.

Some faults in our world, of course, can be explained by claiming that they do not appear evil in God's sight but only in ours. However, surely such an event as a holocaust does not appear good to God in any sense of the word. All our attempts to make evil out to be merely a product of our limited human perspective, unknown as such by God, fail. Either God understands such devastation just as we do, or else he is of no religious service to us in trying to explain that experience.

The notion that such waste of human life somehow serves God's ultimate purpose, at least in any simple way, is equally repugnant. The fully rational God of Descartes, Spinoza, and Leibniz becomes useless to us. Alone, rational principles fail to explain mass destruction, even if appeals to the great benefits derived from experiencing evil may give a plausible account of minor ills. It is hard, if not impossible, to work a holocaust into a rationally devised scheme. We must, then, be dealing with a God whose nature involves a wider latitude than rational principles—if they were to dominate—would allow.

Furthermore, any view of the world's process as being "necessary" or "predestined" by God is not only unhelpful but actually repellent where holocausts are concerned. It is shocking even to consider that God not only knew but plotted such destruction from eternity. We can hide some mysteries in the inscrutability of God's nature and his future plan, but not a holocaust.

Freedom and will become absolutely essential as divine attributes for any picture of a holocaust God. Contingency and chance are equally important. We must be dealing with a God who takes great risks and whose mode of control is at best quite loose. We face a God with a policy of noninterference, one who consciously created men with a greater capacity for evil and destruction than any aim to enhance good could ever account for. And he did this in place of other good options open to him, some more preferable from a human point of view.

Such a God, certainly, is not easy or comfortable to believe in, but that need not be so great a difficulty for organized religion as it might seem. Easy and obvious as Descartes' God is, few have come to believe in him on the basis of rational necessity alone. Once our romantic views of life have been exploded by passing through a holocaust, only a God more difficult to deal with seems likely to account for a harsh world.

Theologians who follow Hegel's lead thought for a long time that God works through advances in culture, primarily Hebraic or Western. But since Western culture has produced some of the greatest holocausts, God must be divorced from any attachment to the achievements of culture. Otherwise, he falls victim to its devastations too. Whatever advantages advanced cultures bring to us, they do not save us from evil. If high cultures really represent God's intentions for man, then God's program will often receive a harsh evaluation.

The highest achievements of culture and science lead as easily to death camps and nausea as they do to a comfortable God and an easy celebration of life. Religious institutions at best get a mixed score as God's representatives in a time of holocaust. God may have his deputies on earth, but it is heroic individuals, and not always those highest in the church hierarchy, who exhibit what we call the spirit of God in the face of destruction. In fact, the higher in church hierarchies the less free do officials seem to be to speak out. They may represent God well in ceremony but not so effectively in the face of destruction.

Does all this mean that Christians must abandon the notion of God as loving or as entering into human life to share it? Not necessarily, but certainly the holocaust does tell us that the meaning of love must be rethought. It is just as much a mystery as it is a pleasure. Romantic love is ruled out where God is concerned, since even intense suffering is not excluded in the divine scheme. Love either does not or perhaps will not always intervene to prevent destruction.

106

God may enter into our human experience, but all overtones of triumphalism in religion must be abandoned. This is partly because God's presence often goes unrecognized, and surely it has little effect on the course of public life and political events. We cannot see an overt example of the notion that God "rules the world." This would have to involve both what we cannot see and the future as yet unrealized, or else we cannot make sense of that idea, given the world around us.

Any God who survives the holocaust will remain largely unseen on the face of history. If we insist on trying to see him there, it can only be during times of triumph, not destruction. Any experience of holocaust returns a sense of mystery to life that can never be dispelled. Furthermore, we must be careful about romanticizing the depth of mystery in our experience of God by saying that it "explains" much. At best, romanticizing postpones understanding; at worst it destroys the possibility of revelation.

The rationalist's impulse is to get rid of all mystery if he can, but that attempt assumes that all phenomena can be given an overt and a rational explanation, which is what Freud thought true of the psyche too. Of course, "mystery" simply means that a final explanation now exceeds our powers, whereas the rationalist posture is that nothing exceeds the grasp of a modern scientifically based reason. The way God operates is something one must be God to fathom fully.

Neither the world nor God is in the grip of any fixed necessity, since what is fixed in its course can be explained without residue or mystery, as Aristotle noted years ago. Instead, our experience tells us that there must be still, in the life of God as well as men, indeterminate events and contingencies which depend on the future decisions of the will. Power must not be clearly assigned to either positive or negative channels if it can spill over into destruction so easily. Rationality thus leads as easily to evil as to good, a possibility the rationalist prefers to deny.

Reason may calculate, but neither in God nor in human

nature does it appear of itself to specify only one right action. We are all capable of setting aside any course of action offered to us, no matter how "good" it may be, and acting in contradiction to it. God's will and power may move with considerable independence from the calculations of his reason. Even his attraction to what is good does not control his decisions in any simple sense. What is simply venturesome must exert some independent attraction on God. It is not the good alone which moves him to act.

Evidently, God moves neither easily nor automatically toward any intervention in our affairs. In this respect, his power of restraint exceeds ours considerably. We need not conclude that God is indifferent to human tragedy, but at least we know he can keep his hand away from physical intervention in our affairs even in the face of extreme need. Whether he is always spiritually present and available to us is another matter. If he is, this may be comforting to some, although it produces no mass effect on all of humanity, only on a few.

If God does work individually and not on the scale of history and cultures, his effect at present is at best minimized or reduced. Ironically, it comes nowhere near the power exercised by tyrants. It is hard to side with a God who binds the use of his own power where destructive evil is concerned, although this precludes neither God's intervention in a more public way in the future nor our acceptance of him at that time. However, a belief in such a possibility does not rest on any evidence of obvious divine intrusion in the past.

In the presence of a holocaust-God, danger always threatens. If we still believe he can or will save us from danger, our faith will have to rest on evidence other than the holocaust. In the midst of destruction, there are some who come to feel even more certain that God supports them, but not in the sense of being removed from danger or spared the loss of life. Some who were part of the Nazi holocaust strangely reported an increasing sense of the closeness of God, but their lives were seldom spared as a result.

The holocaust-God may not himself demand sacrifice in some primitive sense, but evidently he allows it. And his sense of time and urgency cannot be ours. Although he converts some of his decisions to a long-range perspective in the midst of a holocaust, the outward result is still loss or destruction. To live through a holocaust, God obviously has great power and strength of will. The question we are each left to ponder is whether we believe this power to be strong enough to rescue us from the jaws of hell at the world's end. Can we trust in God's unwavering determination to release us with a final stroke?

XIV. GOD IS NOT . . .

ABLE TO SPEAK TO US DIRECTLY

Except to a very few, in the present age God does not seem to "speak" to us, at least in any obvious or ordinary meaning of that term. Still, many claim that God has spoken in the past, and there are individuals who assert that God addresses words to them directly as persons now. The important point is that even if we have heard such words, they are still subject to an element of strangeness. Any voice that is heard but not seen does not come to us in the usual manner.

Whether in individual cases or in sacred literature, the "speaking" of God may be described as the hearing of a voice. Yet any claim to "hear" God is never asserted to be an ordinary case of speaking. Therefore, if we are to explain what we mean when we say that God speaks, we will have to develop a special sense for the term. However, if we want to rely on such unusual "speech," we also need more extensive justification than a mere claim.

Some critics want to restrict us to use only the ordinary meaning of a term, but this limitation involves certain assumptions which we must examine before we accept this restriction. On the opposite side of the argument, it could be said that all insight into our life comes from the extra-ordinary use of terms and that ordinary use yields only common knowledge. Plato felt that a special type of "madness" was not to be regarded as so destructive as we might ordinarily suppose. Quite the contrary, he believed certain kinds of madness could be valuable and an important source of insight.

This might be the case with God and "speaking." That

is, since it is clear that no ordinary use of this term can apply, if we can locate some unusual sense, this might offer us a crucial insight concerning our knowledge of God. In religion we must always be concerned with locating new sources of information. If a way can be found for us to accept any words we hear as God's, that is a source of knowledge we cannot afford to overlook.

The notion that religion must undertake non-ordinary investigations is actually quite suitable. When religion accepts the rationalistic premise that experience must be universal and common, it has more trouble sticking to this limitation than the average secularist. Religion's basic materials involve sacred literature and religious experience. When we examine these, neither unusual meanings (e.g., God speaks) nor extra-ordinary experiences (e.g., miracles) can be avoided. Any attempt to reduce these exceptional experiences to ordinary forms only destroys what religion has to offer that secular life cannot provide.

In what sense, then, will God "speak" if he does so at all? His words are recorded in our accumulated sacred literature, but when these are spoken, some human being is the source. In this case, how did the one who first wrote them down hear the words? The first impression we have is of a multitude of voices each claiming to convey God's messages. This multiplicity of sounds is difficult to reconcile with the idea of one God. We might assume either that God does not wish to speak with one voice or that it is only the human mode of transmission which develops the variety of voices. We assume that God speaks no single dialect or language. However, since men must hear in some particular form, any "divine word" unavoidably takes on the coloring and the complexity of a particular language.

We must ask ourselves what God's reasons might be for making both his communication and the recovery of his meaning such a complicated process; it is all more difficult than is necessary, and in the end no interpretation ever receives universal acceptance. The biblical story of the

Tower of Babel gives us one answer. There God imposed a variety of tongues on us as punishment for arrogance.

In any case, religious followers must explain why we have multiple religious languages and account for why God did not elect to use one of the most adequate and precise technical languages, which men so easily develop, for his important communications. In contrast, God's speaking involves his choice of a complicated and technically inferior (due to its multiplicity of voices) means of communication.

Why isn't God clear and direct? Why doesn't he answer our questions? Why is he sometimes silent? He is silent as to why he did not at the outset install a more efficient universal language and a clear means of communication between the designer and those who receive his words. Furthermore, he has been silent about providing keys and rules for interpreting the non-uniform "messages" attributed to him in a variety of imperfect languages. Since he could easily have spoken more definitively had he wanted to, we can only interpret his silence and inaction as a sign that he preferred to leave us alone to work out our own interpretation without providing us with an absolute guideline.

With a single stroke, God could have saved biblical students centuries of probing and inconclusive results. However, God's "speaking" must contain an irremovable element of silence at crucial points. That is, God has "spoken" by giving us our imperfect plurality of languages. And he has also "spoken" by what he has not done—that is, by neither creating a perfect language nor speaking out directly in order to correct our misinterpretations. Actions speak louder than words—for God too.

In this sense we can say God has spoken to us, since we can learn some of his intentions from examining our situation. For instance, he wished to "speak" in this inconclusive and multiple way, and he does not wish to do so in a simpler and perhaps more perfect manner. Technically, God is silent as far as direct communication goes, but his actions speak for him here. He has left the

able to speak to us directly

details of deciphering his reasons for not speaking in a single authoritative voice to our discovery. Thus, our words about God's words are always subject to a certain imprecision which necessitates our involvement if any interpretation is to come forth.

XV. GOD IS NOT . . .

ABLE TO BE VERY RELIGIOUS

"WHY I AM NOT VERY RELIGIOUS"
(An open letter to the men and women of the world.)

"Although I am often made an object of religious devotion, I have never been able to become fully religious myself. Of course to be 'religious' means many things, and some forms attract me more than others. I have never gone in for elaborateness or formality, although papal pomp is at times spectacularly well done and entertaining to watch. I think what holds me back from the full enjoyment of religious ritual, whether simple or elaborate, is that I cannot lose myself in it completely, as the devout worshiper tends to do.

"This difference, I think, is due to the fact that I have so much on my mind that I cannot afford the luxury of shutting out all except religious devotion. The worshiper may narrow his field of vision, but I must remain constantly aware of the world made up of men and women and children and other living things. The stars and galaxies and every possible universe are always on my mind too. But I think what most of all holds me back from becoming completely religious is the tendency of the human religious consciousness to focus exclusively on the good in the world, while I can never escape the force of evil or block out my painful awareness of the destruction it reaps.

"In societies and cultures the numbers who are religiously inclined vary in proportion to those who are secularly inclined. Much as I admire some who are religious, I can never forget that I am responsible for creating the a-religious population too. Actually, I enjoy secular society a great deal. I could have blocked out such ranges of interest and made the peoples of the world to be like one large church, with constant devotion and round-the-clock religious services. But that perspective seemed a little narrow, not to mention dull, and also a little unfair to the full range of human experience. I blush to confess that I find the pleasures of the nonreligious at times as fascinating as prayer. The dangers and risks involved in various human adventures are attractive to me. I do not think I could be a monk, or a hermit, although I can respect such singlemindedness.

"When the world at large and humanity in general are your concern, you can only devote so much attention to religiousness, important though I consider it. The tendency of the religious consciousness is to create a God who satisfies that image of human desire, but I could not afford to be limited to such an image unless I rejected responsibility for the whole world and all the variety I created within it. Besides, freedom is so central to my nature (although it took theologians a long time to discover this) that I cannot afford to be controlled by priests. And the tendency of all religions is to determine my actions, to tell me what I can and cannot do. I created an openness to change in human existence that I do not want to go back on, partly because openness to novelty is a pervasive tendency in my own nature. I would be false to myself if I tried to deny it.

"Religious writings of course at times catch my nature clearly and make my people aware of me. The religions of the world, when taken together, expand human horizons. They are on the whole a better avenue to me than, say, selfish hedonism. But the problem for church- and temple-goers is not to become too narrow in the process of finding out what religion has to offer. Thus, I can never go too far with one religious form or take sides in religious controversy, because so much of it is simply another form of selfish power politics. I can't afford to endorse any single path as an exclusive access to me, although religious leaders are always trying to force an exclusive endorsement from me. This does not mean that I may not appear or enter into human life or offer signs of my nature, my power, and my intentions. It is just that my own view of these actions remains different from the forms which various religions later give to them.

"My reluctance where religious practice is concerned comes about essentially because I would be false to my complex nature if I endorsed any single religious form or way of life. Such exclusiveness is for men and women but not for Gods. It is for me to propose signs; it is for human beings to give interpretations of my actions. But since to be religious means to narrow oneself down to one form of life or theological interpretation, I can admire men who sacrifice and go that far, but it is not for me to follow them. Of course, I do not find all religions equally attractive. I update my evaluations constantly, since any religion or any human religiosity changes rapidly over time. Some become so unrepresentative of what I consider my central core—love—that it takes great strength not to protest against their speaking in my name. But I keep silent. I let men judge for themselves where they find my presence.

"At times I have thought it would be nice to be a pope or a high church official. I like the drama and the vestments, but I can't afford time away from the world to confine myself solely to ecclesiastical affairs. Still, the outward religious authority these men have is attractive. Since I have myself resisted the temptation to mark out any clear and final line of authority, they do it for me. I do not want to get involved in the human quarrel over who is first or who should speak ex cathedra. True, my full power is always ready in reserve, but I restrain myself and seldom show it. Churches and temples and bishops' houses are nice and sometimes even godly places, but still they are only a small part of the various dwelling places on earth. I must stay constantly open to be in any house, in any place, at any time where I am called or choose to be.

able to be very religious

"Many become religious in order to shut out terror, whether psychological or physical. They want to see only the good in life. I'd like to shut out terror too, with a hymn or a prayer or a beautiful ritual. But terror is so close to me that I face it constantly. I have promised not to let it destroy the whole of creation, although it destroys enough each day to make it impossible for me to avoid grief. Most religions try to shut out uncertainty too, but I must face it. What is more, I rather enjoy the precarious and the unpredictable in life. However, I admit that I hold the power of absolute control, whereas only a few men and women can hold their world on course and then only for a time. I understand the tendency of humans to seek certainty and all-goodness in religion, and I do not blame them. It is just that such assurance and all-goodness is forbidden to me, since I do not want to ignore the full range of my creation.

"Almost all religions form favored groups and then appeal to me to give them special treatment. True, being discriminating by nature, I do not treat all people alike, although I do offer love to all equally. Some religions represent my desires more purely than others. But I must be wary of forming an exclusive identification with any one, for almost as sure as they feel they have my favor, they grow corrupt. Soon you find someone speaking in your name, claiming a special status, whom you would rather not be identified with. The problem is how to give recognition without getting tied into an unbreakable contract; how to use a representative or a group without having them turn such trust into a hammer to hit or destroy their enemies. I would like to trust religions and religious leaders, but, like political power, religion too easily corrupts into an arrogant self-righteousness. A God cannot be too careful with whom he associates or what commitments he makes when dealing with human beings.

"Certainly, the feeling the sincerely religious person has that I can become wholly present to him or her, that their human concern of the moment is also mine, is not false. I can become fully present in a time and place. All

117

that is wrong is that the religious consciousness wants to confine my whole life to that. It holds me exclusively at that place long after my time of presence is past. I must be about my business, and that is why I cannot afford to lead a totally religious life myself. As necessary as religion is for many individuals, it is too restrictive for one who laid the foundations of the world to bind himself to without relief. My heart is as attentive to those who know no religious life as to those who make it their whole life. I must be a God to the secular too—whether they are aware of it or not.

"Perhaps my point would best be summed up if I said: Religion is for men and women, not Gods. Exclusiveness and peace and rest is not a way open to a creator-sustainer being. At the very least, I would have to say that a life devoted fully to religion lies outside my grasp as long as the world lasts. That is, I unleashed the terrors and the powers of destruction from the bonds that hold them in my own nature to allow them a certain scope in my creation. Until such time as these forces are brought back into full control, that is, until the lion lies down with the lamb, I cannot rest.

"Actually religious people are those who look forward to the day when this will happen. The religious are those who, so to speak, live in an ideal world they believe will eventually come on earth. But often they forget that such a new order is not yet here. Forces other than religious devotion are now in control of the world, and some of these constantly threaten us with destruction. I can never afford to forget that. I cannot join the religious in celebrating an expected future day as if it were already here.

"Of course, such a new day is already here in the sense that it lies in my power to bring it about. Most religions are right when they proclaim that I have promised to bring an order of peace into existence. But I am stubborn. I refuse to be pinned down to a precise date. In that sense I know less than some of my religious followers, and I am also less able to join them in advance celebration about a future world I still have not brought about.

"Many groups, both Marxist and Christian, have thought they could themselves usher in this new world, one in which all destruction shall be halted and all wounds healed. They claim to have divined some secrets, and I sometimes feel as if my power had passed into their hands. Actually, the power to remake the world's basic plan is one force I have reserved to myself from creation. Until that strength is brought into play, I cannot relax and be exclusively religious. I hope I have explained why. I blush slightly and thank all religions for the honors they give me, even if I cannot join them just yet.

"Most of what I have said so far involves my personal reasons for not joining any religious organization. If I consider my responsibility to others, my reasons not to unite with, or approve any special privilege for, one religious group over another are that I must hold myself open to be the God of all Christians, of all religions, not just some. Of course, outside the West I have religious interests other than the specifically Christian. More than that, I can't endorse any one Christian theology, because I must remain open to all religious people, Christian or otherwise.

"I do not reject the Christian claim that Jesus represents a special revelation of my nature and my intent. Nor do I believe that all religions are somehow equal and have my uncritical approval. It is just that, once a group gets the feeling that I endorse them exclusively or authorize some one theological view, they tend to become both lax and arrogant. Then they concentrate on preserving their privileged positions rather than on promoting my causes of love and relief for those who suffer. Jesus came preaching my word of love and forgiveness, and men and women have been fighting for control over his message ever since.

"I admit that I had something to do with the vision Peter had soon after the formation of the early Christian church. That is when Peter discovered that I did not send Jesus to the Jews alone, although Jesus was thoroughly Jewish himself, but to all people open to receive my message. The early Christians fought the battle over whether or not to open themselves to the world and to move away from an exclusive Jewishness. They elected nonexclusiveness then, but ever since that day they have simply turned the tables on me and acted as if I now intended a message of love and forgiveness only for members of some Christian sect. I have no objection to the formation of certain churches or groups, and I enjoy some of the worship services, but I do object to organizations' trying to tie my message down to their exclusive control and representation.

"With Jesus as my voice, I tried hard to prevent any tight ecclesiastical structure from forming, or any creedal orthodoxy from establishing itself as if it were my dominant concern. I picked someone without scholarly education, not a part of any establishment, Roman or Jewish. He spoke only orally and authorized no text. Alas, this has not prevented men from trying to tie both Jesus and me down to some fixed verbal statement and formal interpretation, as if that were my primary concern. Jesus worked by action and by loose oral illustration, but human beings seem to require more security than such an informal way of proceeding allows. Of course, their needs are greater than mine and their power is less. Still, I cannot endorse any one religious group or doctrine for fear of simply making matters worse.

"I think of myself as a person of action and not of words only, as a person of compassion and generosity, not one who is narrow. I do not enjoy haggling over who is right and who says things correctly. I do like beauty of expression and simplicity, but my life is too varied; too much of my nature is expressed in a variety of forms and cultures for me to identify myself with only one. Human beings try to reduce everything to a strict unity to enable easy police action against those who challenge them. But I am a pluralist myself. I am not seen equally in all religions, but the process of sifting the true from the false I leave to men and women. It is their human task, and I do wish they would not shift their responsibility to me by claiming that I

able to be very religious

have made them my authorized, exclusive spokesman or issued some definitive religious document. I have enough on my mind without getting involved in religious one-upmanship!"

Yours faithfully,

God*

*Responsible for publication: Frederick Sontag

POSTSCRIPT

Is God As You Like It?

By this time, you may have discovered what God is and what God is not. But, do you like what you have found? Is the God you discovered anything similar to what you think a proper God ought or should be like? Is God meant to satisfy man's every desire, or does he fall short of fulfilling the image we often expect of him? Can the God of religious worship and human desire ever be reconciled with the God who created the world as we find it? Perhaps no one God can satisfy us all. Have you learned more about God than you really care to know? Is ignorance bliss where the secrets of God's life are concerned? Why won't God hold still so that we can approach him easily? Like children with their parents, are we faced with a God who can never quite be all we would like him to be?

Can God be both the God we want and the God he is? I think he can. Certainly he has the power to be both. But the issue is, can we accept him on such difficult terms, since he is no longer just like the God of our dreams? As the Benedictine monk said who appeared at my door in a Roman monastery midway through my first term of lectures: "I now see what your God is like and I don't like him!" We know the kinds of pictures of God which men like to construct when they are free to think in their own way. But if God is not as free as men are to satisfy their desires by constructing a world built of dreams, could God be less than we might like him to be and still accomplish his purpose? In any case, I think we have begun to sketch what God is and what God is not. Perhaps the most amazing thing is that God permits us to do this, that he lets us know anything at all about himself. God is not afraid of discovery, although he certainly hasn't made the process easy for us.

Does God Change Faces?

> Even eternity changes its face.
> Elie Wiesel in *Legends of Our Time*

Confronted with the many faces of God, we have a choice: We can deny that any one face which God offers us is adequate or acceptable (known as atheism); or, we can argue that the one face we find attractive is "the only true way" to see God (sometimes called orthodoxy). Behind all this is the question of whether we are going to accept or reject our assignment to try to reconcile all the various faces of God which men have seen. This is an unending task, and our assurance of God often falls into limbo, but there is no way to force men to accept a difficult path when an easier way is available. God seems to have set an obstacle in the way of our pursuit of him, because the simplest way (that is, either one face of God or none) is not the right way.

If only one face of God were correct (e.g., Descartes' thinking God), or if God could be guaranteed absolutely not to exist, the issue could be settled once and for all. But if in fact God is to be found only among a whole army of faces that men see, not only is the pursuit of God the most difficult task set for men, but it can never be fully completed. Any face of God we begin to build up out of all the pictures of God ever presented to us will be basically unstable and thus capable of no final formulation. To "hold still" any picture we form of God, requires all our human strength and attention. We also know that any time we give up on our effort, the face of God we have discerned among the many will recede from view and lose the strength it once had for us.

Of course, behind this dilemma lies the question: Why would God choose to express himself through many faces rather than one? And if he does this, what does this fact tell us about his nature? That is, is there something in the nature of God that makes many faces, rather than one, a more accurate expression of divinity? In understanding himself God also faces multiplicity, and he remains balanced in nature and in control of his actions only by facing multiplicity, or the threat of disintegration, successfully. Thus, we cannot realize the depth of power in the divine nature if we settle on only one simple and perhaps serene face. To know God in truth we must experience some of his own struggle with the vast heterodoxy of the faces of God. We must understand how his power works to contain this diversity.

Does our insight into "divine division" mean that one can never claim that any revelation of one face or of one divine action either points to a core or governs God's relation to all the possible Gods men know? Can Jesus claim that God's center is compassion and not a demand for religious ceremonial sacrifice? Is that what God really wants? Can Christians claim that Jesus has himself led us to the God among the Gods or to the heart of the matter? Yes, of course. For if the core we locate in multiplicity does not degenerate into the chaos of destructive warfare, we have found a controlling center. But finding such a single center would not have been necessary if we did not have to deal with the many faces of God to begin with.

Similarly, any claim to "revelation" would be meaningless if any one face of God were obviously right from the beginning. The world's religions confront us with many claims, with many faces. But no revelation would be startling if it simply presented us with what every man knew all along. If God cares and expresses his compassion for men by entering into their suffering voluntarily, this idea should be an amazing notion to the human observer caught in both religion's many Gods and in the violence of human action. Faced with a multiplicity of Gods, the diversity of human life, and the complexity of conflicting religious claims, revelation then becomes both meaningful and needed if we are ever to find one face behind the many.

Furthermore, the face revealed to us must not be an obvious one, that is, one that results from simply fixing on one religion's God. Divinity's core must be hidden. Otherwise it would not need to be revealed. God's mode of operation must be esoteric rather than open to all. The easy way of universalism or explicit knowledge open to all does not intrigue God. He must feel a little pang of conscience when he turns down man's request for simplicity and finality. God must never rest. He grants man rest because we humans need it, not because it is an imitation of the divine life. God may have left his "traces" in the world, but it is still very easy to overlook the path to God.

Besides, every face of God men claim to have seen cannot be "true" by itself, and all of them are neither reconcilable nor manageable if compressed into one composite. God is not simply a collage of all his various faces. But if he is not, how do we find a criterion, or the criteria, for accepting or rejecting the various faces of divinity which men offer to us? What provides the central clue that makes it possible to find God among all the Gods without simply indulging in artificial exclusion? The trick, it would seem, is not to discover some fixed notion of God. Instead we should first find the lead characteristic of God, which begins a process of reconciliation and then acceptance of one face and the rejection of others from among the many faces of God. How do we find this clue to God?

Descartes offers reason's self-fulfilling demands as his clue to divinity's core. Jesus offers love and sacrifice. Ecclesiastical hierarchies offer us the institutionalization of God's relations with man. Psychologists offer an inner path, others a spiritual guide. Our test is to ask whether the key insight suggested to us operates by rejecting everything but itself. This is a luxury, we have discovered, that God did not indulge in in creation.

Or, must the key we choose accept all which both religious and secular men have claimed about divinity and go on both to indicate a way to discern a core among the multiplicity and a plan to hold onto that vision? We should begin our quest by demanding that any key to God be able to account for *all* we find in men and in the world, not just part. God's creation of the irreducible multiplicity in which we live must have been intentional and thus be reflective of divinity's core.

DATE DUE

OCT 24 83			
GAYLORD			PRINTED IN U.S.A